Ethics in School Librarianship: A Reader

Edited by
Carol Simpson

Linworth
PUBLISHING, INC

Library of Congress Cataloging-in-Publication Data

Ethics in school librarianship : a reader / edited by Carol Simpson.
    p. cm.
Includes bibliographical references.
 ISBN 1-58683-084-8
 1. School librarians--Professional ethics. 2. School libraries--Moral
and ethical aspects. 3. Library science--Moral and ethical aspects. I.
Simpson, Carol, 1949-
 Z682.35.P75E75 2003
 174'.9092--dc21
                              2003007956

Published by Linworth Publishing, Inc.
480 East Wilson Bridge Road, Suite L
Worthington, Ohio 43085

Copyright © 2003 by Linworth Publishing, Inc.

ISBN: 1-58683-084-8

5 4 3 2 1

Table of Contents

Preface

Creating a work of this sort is incredibly difficult. Not only must you assume that you follow the ethical high road, you must recruit others who feel the same way. In teaching school-librarians-in-training, I have often wished for clear, yet scholarly, discussions of the topics that are so important to novices in the profession. Embracing the ethical precepts that frame and color everything we do in the library is the "mountaintop experience" in becoming a librarian. We didn't become librarians so we could teach reading, or tell stories, or proselytize technology, or surround ourselves with literature, though some or all of those reasons may have entered into our decision to begin our studies. We became librarians because we had a passion for connecting individuals and information, whether that information is facts, or art, or literature. We became *school* librarians because we knew we would be at the forefront of the push to develop lifelong learning and a deep, abiding respect for the building blocks of knowledge — information.

Using This Book

Reading about ethics is no walk in the park. The issues are thorny, and they can cause discomfort. Some of the topics discussed and the positions taken by the various authors may raise your blood pressure. The issues are, however, essential to the profession and thoughtful reading and discussion are essential to the discipline.

Typical uses for this work will be class discussion among students of school libraries and school administration. The individual chapters can be taken as independent readings, or the discussion questions may form the basis for class discussion or individual research papers. Practicing professionals may want to read the entire book for a book study group or to simulate policy-making discussions on the ethical practices of the profession.

The Authors

To know what ethical principles an individual espouses one must follow the individual's career. In writings and speeches, one can get a taste of the ethical compass that guides an individual. The contributors to this volume are diverse. Women and men, academics and practitioners, they are all respected in their fields and are sought after for guidance by students and librarians in the profession. To help you grasp the scope of this assembled group, here are some brief glimpses at their careers and contributions.

Mary Ann Bell, Ed.D., is an Assistant Professor of Library Science at Sam Houston State University in Huntsville, Texas. She received her B.A. from Baylor University, Waco, Texas, and taught reading and English for 10 years. In 1985, she earned an MLS from Sam Houston State University in Huntsville, Texas, and went on to serve for 15 years as a middle school librarian. After earning her Ed.D. from Baylor in 2000, she joined the faculty at Sam Houston State.

Kay Bishop, Ph.D., is an associate professor and Director of the School Library Media Program at the University at Buffalo. She has over 20 years of experience as a school media specialist in both public and private schools and has been a member of the faculty at the University of South Florida, the University of Kentucky, the University of Southern Mississippi, and Murray State University. She has written numerous articles and has co-authored two books dealing with school media librarianship. Dr. Bishop has a particular interest in collection development issues.

Nancy Everhart, Ph.D., is an associate professor and coordinator of the school library media program at St. John's University in New York City. The author of *Evaluating the School Library Media Center* (Libraries Unlimited, 1998), she speaks and writes frequently about evaluation issues. She is the winner of several national awards and is active in the American Association of School Librarians. Her upcoming book, *Controversial Issues in School Librarianship: Divergent Perspectives*, will be published by Linworth.

Carrie Gardner, Ph.D., is the Coordinator of Library Media Services at Milton Hershey School in Hershey, Pennsylvania. She has been the Chair of the Pennsylvania School Librarians Association Intellectual Freedom Committee for 12 years. She has also served as Chair of the AASL Intellectual Freedom Committee and the ALA Intellectual Freedom Round Table. She presents scores of programs and writes on intellectual freedom, privacy, and access to information via electronic means.

Frank Hoffman, Ph.D., is a Professor of Library Science at Sam Houston State University, in Huntsville, Texas. He has authored over 30 books, including *The Development of Collections of Sound Recordings*, *Popular Culture and Libraries*, *Intellectual Freedom and Censorship*, and *The Literature of Rock* series. His teaching responsibilities include library collection development, information services, research methods/ grantsmanship, and interpersonal communications.

Doug Johnson has been the Director of Media and Technology for the Mankato Public Schools since 1991 and has served as an adjunct faculty member of Minnesota State University, Mankato, since 1990. His teaching experience has included work in grades K–12 in schools both here and in Saudi Arabia. He is the author of three books: *The Indispensable Librarian*, *The Indispensable Teacher's Guide to Computer Skills*, and *Teaching Right from Wrong in the Digital Age*. His regular column appears in *Library Media Connection* magazine and his articles have appeared in over 30 books and periodicals. Doug has conducted workshops and has given presentations for over 100 organizations throughout the United States as well as in Malaysia, Kenya, Thailand, Germany, Qatar, and Canada.

Carol Simpson, Ed.D., is an Assistant Professor in the School of Library and Information Sciences and Fellow of the Texas Center for Digital Knowledge at the University of North Texas in Denton. As a public school teacher, librarian, and administrator for 25 years, she has taught every grade from Kindergarten to graduate school. Her research and writing focus on intellectual property issues with a focus on K–12 educational practice, technology use in school libraries, and ethical concepts. She is the author of *Copyright for Schools: A Practical Guide* (Linworth, 2001) and co-author of *Internet for Schools: A Practical Guide* (Linworth, 2000). She has edited four professional journals, the latest being *Library Media Connection.*

Nancy Willard, J.D., has degrees in elementary education, special education, and law. She taught children with behavior difficulties and practiced technology law before focusing attention on issues of legal and ethical issues related to technology in schools. Willard is a Research Associate with the Center for Advanced Technology in Education at University of Oregon and the director of the Responsible Netizen Institute, which disseminates informational materials related to the safe and responsible use of the Internet.

Harry Willems is the consultant and assistant director of the Southeast Kansas Library System in Iola, Kansas. SEKLS is a multi-type system serving 40 school districts, 53 public libraries, and six academic libraries in 14 counties. He has an MLS from Emporia State University, and an M.A. from California State University at Los Angeles. He has been a school librarian, a college history teacher, and an adjunct instructor at Emporia State University School of Library and Information Management.

Chapter One
An Ethical Dilemma
By Carol Simpson

O ver a decade ago, *School Library Journal* dowager editress Lillian Gerhardt wrote a series of editorials on the recently adopted American Library Association (ALA) Code of Ethics. While the American library community had operated under several codes of ethics dating back as far as 1939, she pointed out several flaws of reasoning behind the 1981 revision and called for revisions to the revisions to fill in, as she put it, "obvious gaps" (Gerhardt, 1990a). Central to her knowing what was in the Code of Ethics was an understanding of what ethics is and how it is applied to a particular profession.

Naturally, one must go backward to understand the concept of ethics. Originating with the Greek word *ethos*, meaning character, ethics follows only philosophy in guiding a profession. Philosophy gives a profession its foundation, whereas ethics gives the profession its walls. Most trace contemporary ethics to the writings of Immanuel Kant who wrote, "Treat every human person whether in your own person or that of another as an end and never merely as a means" (Froehlich, 2000, 264). Essentially Kant was making a case for the golden rule.

Professional ethics, however, extend far beyond the "do unto others ..." philosophy. Bayles offers a set of professional values: freedom and self-determination; physical safety; equal opportunity; privacy; and fundamental well-being (1989). Froehlich addressed these professional ethical essentials in his discussion of ethical codes and intellectual freedom and access to information. He reports "... ethical principles are called into play when deliberating about values, particularly when values may run into conflict ... and when one value may take priority over another" (2000, 267). When one is forced to defend one's profession and one's program, it is quite likely that the values of various stakeholders will clash. Karen Adams defines professional ethics as "rule ethics, as they prescribe an external standard for the conduct of one's profession." She continues, "Professional codes of ethics give practitioners material for internal reflection to encourage self-criticism by the practitioner" (2001, 7). Lindsey finds that a code of ethics is reflective of a profession's attitude toward service and the responsibility it feels toward the clients it serves (1985).

Professional codes of ethics have become so basic that no fewer than 27 countries have listed their librarian codes of ethics on the International Federation of Library Associations and Institutions (IFLA) Web page at <www.ifla.org/faife/ethics/codes.htm>. The American Library Association has established a Code of Ethics for the profession in the United States. Analogous to the codes of ethics established by the National Education Association or the American Medical Association, the ALA's statement of principles shapes the practice of the profession in its political arena. In Canada, The Canadian Library Association has a similar document. Affiliates of the American Library Association, such as the Texas Library Association or the Oklahoma Library Association, may merely adopt the code of the parent organization, or they may add their own interpretations based on state laws affecting library practice.

Mark Frankel reports three different types of ethical codes: aspirational codes that promulgate ideals, educational codes that explain themselves with expository statements, and regulatory codes that govern professional conduct (1989). A combination of aspirational and educational, the ALA Code of Ethics has been revised several times since Gerhardt took on Goliath in her editorials. The latest revision was in 1995 (with an explanatory statement passed in 2001). However, the concepts presented in the Code are central to the profession and have remained unchanged since 1939, save for changes in wording meant to clarify the concepts to both the profession and to the public. In fact, the preface of the 1981 version states: "Since 1939, the American Library Association has recognized the importance of codifying and making known to the public and the profession the principles which guide librarians in action" (ALA, 2002). These principles are the heart and the foundation of the profession. They are the tenets that one adopts to become part of the profession. Whether you agree with all the political machinery of the ALA or not, the founding principles remain the same. This is what librarianship is all about.

Many Hats, Many Points of View

The school library is not only affected by the ethical code of the American Library Association, however. Both the American Library Association and the Association for Educational Communications and Technology (AECT) are responsible for the national standards set for the profession. Both ALA and AECT have highly considered and carefully worded statements of ethics. While not completely parallel, there are distinct similarities between the two codes. As members of the faculty, school librarians are educators. In fact, many, if not most, school librarians are also credentialed teachers. Since teachers have their own codes of ethics, librarians have now assumed yet another mantle of ethical responsibilities under which to labor. Adding personal and religious ethical values to the mix yields a melting pot of behaviors that may be in total conflict.

Taking on multiple ethical frameworks assumes that all the codes have similar goals and intentions. Since each of these roles has its own point of view, it is reasonable to expect there will be times when the various roles will conflict. What the National Education Association perceives as appropriate behavior for a teacher to follow when communicating with parents, for example, may be diametrically opposed to what the American Library Association endorses as ethically correct practice. The many state library associations and state education groups each have some type of statement of ethical behaviors that may or may not be congruent with that of its national cousin.

Knowing the ethical framework of a profession gives members of that profession a playing field and rulebook. Can you imagine the medical profession without the Hippocratic Oath? The entire subset of medical ethics stems from that short, simple mission statement for the profession. Alas, librarianship, and more specifically school librarianship, has no such concise statement. *Information Power* gives us standards, but it doesn't give us ethics.

Many people disagree with their profession's code of ethics. Interestingly, however, the longer-acknowledged professions, such as medicine, law, the priesthood, and the military, have far less dissension about ethical baselines than does librarianship. In those professions, generally only new advances in technology produce loud and animated debate about the application of ethical principles. For example, cloning—a cutting edge technology—has stirred extensive debate in medical, legal, and ecclesiastical circles over the ethics of the practice. The law finds ample debate fodder when new technologies are applied to old legal understandings. Apparently, business has not arrived at a generally accepted code of ethics when one considers the recent accounting scandals and insider trading reports. Interestingly, in January 1990, Lillian Gerhardt wrote:

> The word 'ethics' is on every newspaper's front page and in the lips of every newscaster. This ethical din arises from grand scale thievery by legislators and stock manipulators and all the many commissions created to scrutinize big money scandals. It really ignores the fact that ethics go beyond monotonous, Gargantuan greed (1990a, 4).

Ethics, at the bottom line, is simply the character of the profession. It is what one may count on, what one finds true and right, what one believes. It is the religion of the practice. While even true believers may quibble over the details, the basic concepts stay rooted. This is the ethic of the profession. See more about this topic in "A Hat Trick" in the Appendix.

There are naysayers in any group. Robert Hauptman has taken the role of one who promulgates a contrarian view of the ALA Code of Ethics. He finds that one should pay more attention to one's personal ethical beliefs than to a rigid and possibly compromised code. He states: "To act ethically is to consider basic principles, a course of action, and the potential results, and then to act in a responsible and accountable way. The ethical professional does not simply follow the mandates and fiats of the controlling organization or ethos, especially since the rules are sometimes formulated to protect the practitioner and not the client" (2002, 13).

The High and the Low of It

There are several views of most ethical codes. Librarianship is no exception. One might describe them as "high ethics" and "low ethics" or "perceptual ethics" and "survival ethics." The profession without question embraces some ethical concepts. Resistance to censorship is generally one of the most accepted. However, along with a resistance to improper *removal* of materials from the library should go a resistance to *adding* improper materials to the collection by those who would promote a specific point of view. Nonetheless, this important distinction is not even mentioned in the 1989 Code of Ethics (Gerhardt, 1990b). One might consider that "high ethics" is a broad view of an ethical precept as applied to all aspects of the profession. "Low ethics" would be the application of the ethical principle with a strong dose of reality thrown in. Bodi finds that ethics is ambiguous because there are wars among competing interests (1998). The fact may be, however, that it is competing ethics that cause the problem.

In teaching school-librarians-in-training, I teach a course in audiovisual production. One of our nonprint learning experiences is to play a simulation game. This isn't a typical computer-based simulation, this is a face-to-face game from Simulation Training Systems called *Where do you draw the line?*® In this game, students are presented with an ethical dilemma, and they have to decide to what degree the action they have witnessed is acceptable. They make these decisions while divided into several groups. They decide the acceptability of these actions viewed from the perspectives of the public, business leaders, and themselves. In looking at their assessments, it is always interesting to see that each group finds itself to be more moral, more ethical, than the general public or business leaders. However, the real turmoil sets in when the different groups come together to compare assessments. They are astounded that others might have different perceptions of the witnessed actions than they, themselves, have! When it is revealed that each group had slightly different scenarios to view, they are immediately relieved. Ah, they reason, the others are not different from us or we from them. It was that they had something different to analyze. In reality, though, each of the scenarios involved the same wrongdoing. One set involves theft, another bribery, and so on, and all were for similar amounts or degrees. The groups clash when the discussion turns to intent. Certainly, theft for the purpose of giving to charity is acceptable, while theft for the purpose of personal enrichment is not! Alternatively, is bribery OK in order to get what you want as long as no one gets hurt?

"Ethics matters because it helps us to act responsibly" (Hauptman, 2002, 139). Not having a standard by which to judge is the ethical dilemma. Without such a standard, we are free to apply ethics from other value systems, other aspects of our lives, and we all view things differently. A shared set of values gives us a basis on which to coalesce as a profession, a community. It also gives us a set of standards against which to judge the professional behavior of our peers. As Lillian Gerhardt wrote: "You can't accept reproach if you don't know why what you've done is reprehensible" (1996, 4).

Works Cited

Adams, K. G. (2001). "Ethics in librarianship: an overview." *PNLA Quarterly*. 65(3), 6–7.

American Library Association. (2002). *History of the Code of Ethics: Statement on Professional Ethics*. Retrieved April 2003 from <http://www.ala.org/Content/NavigationMenu/Our_Association/ Offices/Intellectual_Freedom3/Statements_and_Policies/ Code_of_Ethics/History1/Default2090.htm>.

Association for Educational Communications and Technology. (2001). *Code of ethics*. Retrieved on March 6, 2003, from <http://www.aect.org/About/Ethics.htm>.

Bayles, M. D. (1989). *Professional ethics*. (2nd ed.). Belmont, CA: Wadsworth.

Bodi, S. (1998). "Ethics and information technology: some principles to guide students." *The Journal of Academic Librarianship*, 24, 459–63. Retrieved from Library Literature and Information Science Full Text.

Frankel, M. (1989). "Professional codes: why, how, and with what impact?" *Journal of Business Ethics*. 8(2–3), 109–115.

Froehlich, T. J. (2000). "Intellectual freedom, ethical deliberation and codes of ethics." *IFLA Journal* 26(4), 264–72.

Gerhardt, L. N. (1990a). "Ethical back talk: chewing on ALA's Code." *School Library Journal*. 36(1), 4.

Gerhardt, L. N. (1990b). "Ethical back talk: II." *School Library Journal* 36(3), 4.

Gerhardt, L. N. (1996). "Nuts in May: wedded to confidentiality: the Unabomber and you." *School Library Journal* 42(5), 4.

Hauptman, R. (2002). *Ethics and librarianship*. Jefferson, NC: McFarland.

International Federation of Library Associations and Institutions. (2002). *Professional codes of ethics/conduct. International Federation of Library Associations and Institutions*. Retrieved December 15, 2002 from <www.ifla.org/faife/ethics/codes.htm>.

Kant, I. (1959). *Foundations of the metaphysics of morals*. Translated by L.B. White. New York: Library of Liberal Arts. Quoted in: Froehlich, Thomas J. (2000). Intellectual freedom, ethical deliberation and codes of ethics. *IFLA Journal* 26(4), 264-72.

Lindsey, J. A., & Prentice, A. E. (1985). *Professional ethics and librarians*. Phoenix: Oryx.

Discussion Questions

1. Robert Hauptman said, "The ethical professional does not simply follow the mandates and fiats of the controlling organization or ethos." If every librarian were to establish his or her own ethical code, what problems do you foresee for the practice of the profession?

2. In looking at the ALA/AASL Code of Ethics, which aspects are perceptual and which are survival? Justify your opinions.

3. Hauptman states, "Ethics matters because it helps us act responsibly." Can you give an example of when a librarian might not act responsibly? If you cannot identify a situation in which it might be possible for a librarian to act irresponsibly, can you make a case that there is no need for a code of ethics for the profession?

Chapter Two
Ethical Issues in Collection Development

By Kay Bishop

David is a new media specialist at Lincoln High School. He is preparing his first book order and has been reading reviews in professional journals to make his book selections. A reviewer highly recommends a book dealing with gay/lesbian sexual orientations, but David is concerned that a book on this topic might be controversial. He does not want to have people complaining about books in the media center, especially during his first year at the school. Thus, he decides not to order the book.

Janet, a media specialist at First Street Elementary School, has a huge backlog of audiovisual materials that needs cataloging. She has no clerical help, and it seems as if she can never get to tasks such as the cataloging of audiovisual materials. The school district has a union catalog, but Janet has not been able to find any other school that has some of the audiovisual materials she has. Although she has tried to select Dewey numbers from the Abridged Dewey that she keeps in her media center office, the process is slow and some of the items do not seem to exactly fit into the Dewey decimal categories. She feels she cannot take any more time with the task and decides to use some Dewey numbers that seem to be "in the ballpark" and begins to enter them into the union catalog.

Lilly, a media specialist at Willow Middle School, has embarked on a large weeding project since the media center has not been thoroughly weeded for several years and is running out of shelf space. The science section has many outdated books; some even contain inaccurate information, but they are still in good physical condition. Lilly hates to see books "go to waste" and decides to give them to the sixth grade science teachers who have been trying to build up classroom collections.

An irate parent has just returned Maurice Sendak's *In the Night Kitchen* to the media center at Winsor Academy, where Maria is the media specialist for the K–12 private school. The parent, who is on the school board, has informed Maria that he does not want his kindergarten child seeing nudity in books. The parent wants Maria to remove the book from the collection. Maria listens patiently to the parent's concerns, shows him the media center's policy on selection, and explains that although the parent certainly has the right to oversee his child's reading, other parents may not feel the same way about this particular book. The parent, however, is still very concerned about the book and suggests a compromise — drawing some diapers on the nude child in the illustrations. Maria, not wanting any further confrontations, reluctantly agrees, picks up a permanent marker from her desk, and begins drawing blue diapers on Sendak's small boy character.

Justin, the media and technology specialist in the media center at Bradford High, has located a great software program that he thinks will be useful for the ninth grade social studies teachers and students. He purchased rights to only one copy of the program, but he really wants to try it out to see how well the students and teachers like the program. A ninth grade class is about to come into the media center so Justin loads the program onto several computers in order for the students to use it for the research projects on cultures that they do each year. He will then solicit their reactions to the program.

Have David, Janet, Lilly, Maria, and Justin acted ethically as professional media specialists? The answer in all cases is "no." Every day media specialists make ethical decisions that relate to collection development. In some instances, the media specialists are not aware of the ethics behind their decisions, while in other instances, for various reasons they make decisions that ethically (and sometimes legally) are not appropriate.

What Constitutes Collection Development?

Often school library media specialists mistakenly consider the selection of materials to be the only aspect of collection development. Although certainly an important part, there are many other policies and procedures that should be involved in collection development. Van Orden and Bishop define the *collection program* as the processes that are used to both develop and maintain a collection (2001, 23). These processes include knowing one's existing collection and knowing the school community; evaluating and selecting materials and equipment that will support and enrich the curriculum of a school and meet the needs of the students and teachers; acquiring and making materials and equipment accessible to patrons; maintaining and preserving materials and equipment; and evaluating the collection. In order to make sound educational and ethical decisions, policies and procedures should be in place for all of these processes. Several of the items addressed in the American Library Association's Code of Ethics, which was adopted by ALA in 1995, deal with areas of collection development. The ALA Code will be cited in some instances as the ethics involved with collection development are discussed in this chapter.

Knowing the Existing Collection

Much knowledge of a collection is gained by working with the collection on a day-to-day basis, but a media specialist coming into a school must take time to learn as much as possible about a collection before embarking on the other processes that are included in collection development. Time spent browsing the collection, entering searches on a variety of topics into an OPAC, checking copyright dates on materials, learning how to operate equipment, and reading as many materials as possible are all ways a media specialist can begin to acquire information about an existing collection. Without such information, it is difficult to make appropriate and fiscally responsible selection decisions or to assist users with reading advisory or informational questions. Since the primary purpose of a school media center is to adequately serve its users, it is essential for a media specialist to place high priority on knowing the existing collection.

Knowing the School and Community

A school media specialist has a responsibility to know the community and school population before making decisions dealing with the selection of materials for a collection. As in any library, the materials in a school media center should meet the needs of its patrons. Without having knowledge of library users, a media specialist is not able to make wise or ethical decisions regarding what materials to include in a media center. This knowledge should include basic background about the community (socioeconomic status, political and social characteristics, and opportunities to obtain information from other institutions, such as public or university libraries or museums) as well as knowledge relating to the school community (size of classes, abilities of students, ethnic make-up of the school population, instructional needs, and emphases on particular subjects).

Selecting Materials and Equipment

Some of the most important ethical matters for school media specialists are involved with the selection of materials and equipment for a school media center. Selection policies and procedures should uphold intellectual freedom for all the library's users. ALA's Code of Ethics addresses this topic: "We uphold the principles of intellectual freedom and resist all efforts to censor library resources" (ALA, 1995). While intellectual freedom is the subject of another chapter in this book, we would be remiss not to at least discuss it briefly in this chapter dealing with collection development. All media specialists have an ethical responsibility to have a commitment to intellectual freedom. This involves more than simply stating in a policy manual that intellectual freedom is upheld. It means the media specialist must consistently adhere to policies and procedures outlined in the selection of materials as well as in any challenges to the collection. This is often one of the most difficult tasks of a media specialist since (1) media specialists usually bring their own biases, interests, and concerns to the selection process, and (2) most media specialists would like to avoid the emotional confrontations that accompany challenges to materials in a media center.

Separating one's biases and interests when making collection selections is not easy for many media specialists. Again quoting from ALA's Code of Ethics it is essential that "We do not advance private interests at the expense of library users, colleagues, or our employing institutions" and that "We distinguish between our personal convictions and professional duties and do not allow our personal beliefs to interfere with fair representation of the aims of our institutions or the provisions of access to their information resources" (ALA, 1995).

Purchasing books about antiques for the school media collection because the assistant principal wants to sell some of his personal antiques and is interested in finding their worth is not an ethical selection decision. Nor is it ethical to not purchase books dealing with capital punishment because a media specialist is strongly opposed to such a measure. Media specialists must be diligent in putting aside any biases or possible personal gains for themselves or a particular faculty or staff member when deciding which materials or equipment to purchase. If one is not able to set aside certain personal convictions, such as opposition to capital punishment or abortion, when making selections for a collection, then that person should perhaps consider whether the profession of school librarianship is an appropriate choice. We cannot uphold intellectual freedom and at the same time expect everyone to share our feelings on controversial issues. If we are committed to intellectual freedom, then our media center selections must reflect others' views as well.

The author of this chapter once was employed in a school media position following a media specialist who had worked in a high school media center for many years. The collection held an inordinately large number of books on after-death experiences, Gothic novels, and mysteries by British writers. However, very few books that would be considered young adolescent literature were in the collection, and most of those were older titles. In addition, in a "back room" of the media center, which was used as a teacher workroom and housed a very small professional library, two book carts of adult fiction titles were found. Signs on the carts noted the books were to be checked out only by teachers. Taking into consideration the quotes from the ALA Code of Ethics, did the previous media specialist make ethical selection decisions? The answer is a resounding "no." While the educational emphases of a school and the personal interests of students might be observed when examining a media center collection, the personal interests and biases of the media specialist (or particular faculty members) should not be ascertainable.

In the author's experiences of teaching pre-service school media specialists, she has found that students are frequently either (1) "on fire" and ready to defend intellectual freedom in all cases and to include any book on any topic in the collection or (2) not willing to select books that might be controversial or invite a challenge. Realistic and ethical selection decisions should be made somewhere between these two views. Not every book needs to be in a collection. However, it is important to remember that a collection should reflect the curriculum and personal needs of the students as well as the instructional needs of the faculty. The selections should also be age-appropriate. A novel might be suitable for a high school media center collection, but because of its content, might be totally inappropriate for an elementary school collection. This is where the professional training of a media specialist should be applied. If a media specialist is working in a K–12 school where only one collection serves the entire school population, these types of selection decisions can be quite challenging.

The area of selection that frequently raises ethical considerations is self-censorship by the media specialist. Sometimes self-censorship is intentional, as in the case of David, described in the opening paragraph of this chapter, who did not order a book on gay/lesbian sexual orientations because he did not want to include any material in the media center that could be controversial. Controversial materials can be books, videos, newspapers, graphic novels, or magazines that are popular with today's teens. Media specialists who are new to the field must be cautious and must not fall into a self-censorship pattern such as David's. One must admit, however, that dealing with material challenges can be quite emotional, especially in situations such as the one described early in the chapter where Maria agreed to draw diapers on an illustrated character to appease the board member of a private school. In fact, challenges are rarely "cut and dry" situations, even when policies and procedures relating to them are in place, but without such policies and procedures, a challenge can turn into a librarian's worst nightmare.

Sometimes self-censorship is not for reasons of possible controversial materials, but rather, the media specialist questions the materials' literary quality. In these cases, a collection might not include any Hardy Boys or Nancy Drew books, Stines' *Goosebumps*, graphic novels, or young romance novels that are popular with teenage girls. The question of *quality* versus *demand* has been debated in many library circles, but somewhere between these views lies the professional school media specialist's ethical decision to include a realistic balance of the two types of materials.

Some media specialists also claim they do not realize that their selection decisions constitute self-censoring. Although this may be true, it is more likely the media specialist has not consciously considered his or her own biases or interests. This is an ethical essential when upholding intellectual freedom and taking part in the selection process of a school media center.

Acquisition of Materials and Equipment

One might wonder what possible ethical considerations could be encountered when acquiring materials or equipment for a school media center. There are, in fact, a few that come to mind.

After selecting materials and equipment (utilizing criteria specified in a collection development policy), a media specialist then decides which vendor to use for purchasing items. In some instances, an identical book or piece of equipment might be available from more than one jobber or vendor. When selecting a jobber for books or magazines or a vendor for equipment, a media specialist also needs to take into consideration some type of established criteria, such as the discount involved and the quality of service that is provided. Sometimes jobbers or vendors may try to entice a media specialist to purchase from them by providing a personal gift. This can be done through the mail, but more often, it occurs at conferences. In some instances, media specialists attending a conference are invited to special luncheons, receptions, or even quite elegant dinners by vendors hoping to obtain media specialists as customers for their products or services or as a thank you for buying their products. The author of this chapter has attended and enjoyed such functions and has picked up small personal gifts, such as canvas tote bags at conference exhibits, but one must be careful when deciding on a jobber or vendor and must make decisions based on appropriate reasons — because they provide excellent service or a substantial savings for the school, not because there is some type of personal gain or pleasure for the media specialist.

In some instances personal gain for the media specialist might not be involved in an acquisition decision. I can recall one situation in a private school where a media specialist felt obligated, if not somewhat pressured, to purchase media center equipment from the business of an influential parent. If a substantial savings is involved and the quality of the product is not in question, making such purchases might be acceptable, but the opportunity to make an unethical decision is definitely present in such a situation. In all schools, public or private, criteria for purchases should be clearly written into a policy manual so the "right" acquisition decisions can be made.

Goehner notes other ethical issues that librarians need to consider when doing business with vendors (1991). Some vendors experience serious dilemmas caused by librarians, including: defaulting on contracts; abusing policies on book returns; over-encumbering and overspending by libraries; and expecting financial support from vendors for activities that are not related to the library.

Agreements between a school and a vendor should always be put in writing. The school has an ethical obligation to honor any contract or promise made to a vendor. Publishers usually have book return policies; keeping books longer than a publisher's return agreement can cause financial difficulties for the company. Generally, media specialists order books processed to their specifications so if a media specialist overspends a budget, this again produces a dilemma for a vendor. Media specialists have an ethical obligation to keep track of funds spent or encumbered in order to avoid such situations. Finally, vendors should not be asked to donate to school causes that are not related to the library. If both vendors and school media specialists are open and candid with each other, they will be able to gain a better understanding of how to ethically and effectively conduct their business dealings (Goehner, 1991).

Making Materials and Equipment Accessible

ALA's Code of Ethics states, "We provide the highest level of service to all library users through appropriate and usefully organized resources; equitable service policies; equitable access; and accurate, unbiased, and courteous responses to all requests" (ALA, 1995). Once materials are acquired, a media specialist must make them accessible to students and faculty. This again can involve some ethical decisions. Not taking the time to organize materials so that students and faculty can easily access the materials would violate this policy. Because of the large number of tasks involved with being a media specialist coupled with a lack of clerical assistance, some media specialists tend to put the cataloging of materials on a back burner — sometimes for months. Although the materials may be on the shelf, their accessibility is seriously hindered by not having information relating to them in the card catalog or OPAC. The school media center OPAC is increasingly accessible from not only classrooms, but also from students' and faculty members' homes. The absence of information in an OPAC will lead these patrons to believe the items they are seeking are not available in the media center. A similar problem results for users when MARC records are left in an OPAC after materials have been lost or weeded. In these cases, patrons may think materials are available, when they are not.

Another cataloging situation that may involve ethical consideration was described in a scenario at the beginning of this chapter. Janet, the media specialist in an elementary school with a large backlog of audiovisual materials, decided to save time and entered into the school district's union catalog information that she thought was "in the ballpark." In this situation, where other schools are using information in a catalog and perhaps copying it for their records, it behooves a media specialist to make extensive efforts to catalog items accurately. Yes, time is a factor for almost all school media specialists, but when any librarian puts information into a shared catalog, there is an ethical obligation to make the information as accurate as possible.

Some school media centers also are participating in resource sharing with other media centers or libraries. This, of course, increases the accessibility for users of a media center, but resource sharing also entails its share of ethical decisions and obligations. Some of these ethical considerations deal with the amount of copying and sharing that can be done through interlibrary loans. A group known as the National Commission on New Technological Uses of Copyrighted Works (CONTU) provides guidelines for interlibrary loans. These guidelines describe procedures that should be followed in interlibrary loan copying to assure compliance with copyright laws. Although most academic librarians are diligent in following the guidelines, some school media specialists do not follow the guidelines and may not even be aware of them. Ignorance of copyright laws is neither professionally excusable nor can it be used as a legal defense. A media specialist has the ethical responsibility to stay informed on copyright issues.

Many schools now purchase access to online databases. These databases are generally licensed only for students and teachers in a specified school or school district. If there is shared funding provided and the libraries involved are part of the same system, then copying an article for another library in the system would be considered intralibrary loan. In such a case, the fair use guidelines of making a single copy for a patron for a nonprofit purpose is allowable. However, if a request for an item is made from another school media center, which is not commonly funded, and that item is located in an electronic database, it is neither legal nor ethical to copy it for a teacher or student at the other school. This is an area of copyright that media specialists should not only heed themselves, but they also have an ethical responsibility to educate teachers and students on such restrictions. More information on resource sharing, CONTU guidelines, and restrictions and responsibilities related to electronic resources are addressed in the chapters dealing with copyright and access.

Technology has been especially beneficial in making information accessible in school media centers. Internet access has opened a wealth of resources to students and teachers conducting research. However, Internet access has also created many problems with the possibility of students entering inappropriate Web sites. Having students sign acceptable use agreements for Internet access, as well as for other areas of technology, is highly recommended. Such a policy not only helps the media specialist make responsible decisions relating to technology but also guides students in the ethical use of technology.

In their eagerness to make technology available to students, media specialists, however, must be careful to make legal and ethical decisions. In a scenario in the opening paragraphs, Justin loaded a computer software program on several computers to determine if he should purchase more licenses for the program. Even though his intentions may have been good, by doing so, he violated copyright law and made an unethical decision. Such a situation could have been avoided by contacting the software company for written permission or by asking the company if several students could access the program online for a trial period.

Media specialists have a responsibility to provide equal access to all students, including those who speak English as a second language, a growing population in the United States. This can be accomplished by providing resources that help the students learn English as well as materials in the students' native languages. As Harriet Selverstone, an AASL president notes, "We must be concerned with multiculturalism and all that it entails: ethnicity, nationality, gender inequities, social class, and language ... We need to be certain that our collection reflects a cultural representation of our students, that we have unbiased print and electronic material and have collections representative of the various languages spoken by our students" (2001, 5).

There are also numerous ways in which media specialists can make both equipment and materials equally accessible to students with physical or learning disabilities and can make certain the requirements of the Americans with Disabilities Act are being met. Providing physical and intellectual access to students who speak English as a second language and to students with physical and learning disabilities are indeed important aspects of ethical decision making in collection development. More detailed discussions of these topics can be found in the chapter that deals with access.

Maintaining and Preserving the Collection

Every day media specialists make decisions that relate to the maintenance and preservation of materials and equipment. With tight school media center budgets, a media specialist needs to provide conditions that best maintain the collection. Teaching students how to properly care for books and other materials is one area of maintenance responsibility. Storing books loosely on shelves and keeping them dusted regularly also helps maintain the collection. Teachers and students should be trained in the proper operation and care of equipment, and the media specialist needs to check equipment regularly for any possible problems, especially those that might present safety hazards. Televisions and VCRs need to be tightly fastened to carts and should not be moved by students.

Another consideration that affects the maintenance of a collection is the provision of a copy machine so students can make copies. This will deter temptations to tear pages out of books or magazines. Copy capabilities should be made at a reasonable cost to students and should not be used to make a profit for the media center.

If loss of materials is great, the media specialist may need to consider the purchase of a security system. However, before doing so and even after such a purchase, efforts should be made by all members of a faculty to educate students in regard to their responsibilities in the use of media center materials.

Making certain that proper lighting and temperature are maintained in the media center is another responsibility of the media specialist. Too much light, heat, or humidity can damage both materials and equipment. Fulfilling this responsibility generally involves collaboration with school custodians and the administration. Failing to make appropriate, ethical decisions in these areas can do irreparable, expensive damage as media specialists in humid areas of Florida can attest to when air conditioning is left off over summer vacations.

Weeding, or de-selecting materials, is another means of maintaining a collection. By removing unused and worn materials from a collection, an atmosphere of order and care is created. Unfortunately, some media specialists avoid de-selection procedures for a variety of excuses and reasons. One of the most significant barriers to de-selection is a psychological one. Most media specialists have great respect for books, magazines, and other printed materials; thus, it is difficult for school media specialists to dispose of materials. Some media specialists also fear that they might make a mistake by disposing an item that someone soon after will request. Another barrier can be political—administrators, parents, or faculty members can be adamant in their opposition to de-selection. In these cases, the media specialist may need to educate others on the reasons for weeding a collection. Additional barriers or excuses for not weeding a collection include time and lack of personnel. Both of these are practical barriers that media specialists must face and attempt to overcome, even if it means asking for some temporary staff or volunteers to assist with the de-selection process. Neglecting the weeding of a collection for any of the reasons listed is neither ethical nor professional. De-selection is a function that does not exist in isolation, but is an essential part of collection development. To maintain a vibrant, relevant collection, a media specialist should have professional de-selection policies based on established criteria and must be diligent in following a procedure to properly remove weeded materials from the collection.

Just as in other areas of collection development, policies and procedures relating to the maintenance and preservation of the collection need to be written and shared with teachers, administrators, and students.

Evaluating and Reevaluating the Collection

A final area of collection development that creates ethical decision making is the evaluation and reevaluation of the collection. Media specialists are responsible for not only selecting materials and equipment but also for evaluating the collection to make certain it is meeting the needs of users. Various means can be used for evaluation. One method is to provide surveys to teachers and students to determine if the materials they need for research or to support the curriculum are available to them. Such surveys should also include opportunities for specific titles or topics to be recommended for purchase.

Media specialists can use formal methods of evaluating a collection, such as keeping track of the statistics on how often materials and equipment are checked out or utilized in the media center or checking the collection against recommended lists of titles or basic subject lists. Standard lists and bibliographies that are frequently used for evaluating a collection include *Children's Catalog*, *Middle School Catalog*, and *Senior High Catalog* (H.W. Wilson) and *Elementary School Library Collection* (Brodart). It is important, however, to determine whether a title in such a bibliography meets the unique needs of a media center. Analyzing the interlibrary loan requests to determine what materials users were not able to find in the local collection will also help identify needed titles.

A technique called *collection mapping* can be utilized to analyze a collection in relation to the curricular areas of a school and the number of students who are enrolled in courses. Collection mapping provides a graphic representation of the collection and helps a media specialist determine the strengths and weaknesses of the collection in relation to the curriculum.

A physical examination of the collection is also useful for evaluation purposes. This can be done informally by browsing through the collection, or a more formal method can be established where planned efforts are made to determine the size, scope, and depth of a collection. Sometimes media specialists carry out such a procedure when they perform an annual inventory of a collection, or they may set aside a specified time to evaluate the collection. It is helpful if faculty members can assist by examining specific subject areas of the media collection. This is particularly true in high schools where it may be difficult for a media specialist to be an expert in all areas of the curriculum.

A school's curriculum can change or users' needs may change; thus, a reevaluation of materials is necessary. Not keeping abreast of such changes and not applying reevaluation methods to the collection are not in keeping with the ethical responsibility of meeting the needs of the patrons.

De-selection of materials or weeding must again be considered when evaluating a collection. If materials are no longer needed in a collection or if materials contain inaccurate information, those items need to be removed from the collection. Media specialists must take care to ethically dispose of such materials. In one of the scenarios in the opening paragraphs of this chapter, Lilly weeded old science books from her collection, but offered those titles, which contained inaccurate information, to teachers for their classroom collections. Such a procedure is not ethical. If materials contain incorrect information, they should be disposed of in such a way that they will not be utilized again. In some school districts, certain restrictions are placed on the disposal of media center materials. For instance, in a school district in Florida where the author of this book was employed as a media specialist, weeded materials could not be given directly to students even though the school had many high-need students. All weeded materials had to be donated to nonprofit organizations. Thus, the media specialist made the decision to donate all useable books to local boys and girls clubs and other nonprofit youth organizations.

As in other areas of collection development, evaluation and re-evaluation of materials and equipment should be covered with policies and procedures that guide a media specialist in making responsible, ethical decisions.

Conclusion

Collection development involves numerous ethical decisions that media specialists make on a daily basis. In order to make appropriate decisions, media specialists need to educate themselves in areas of the curriculum, special needs of students, and educational trends and issues; in copyright laws and guidelines; and in methods of meeting the requirements of the Americans with Disabilities Act. They must consistently uphold the principles of intellectual freedom and intellectual property rights. They should subscribe to fairness in buying resources and should acquire materials in a variety of formats. They must strive to provide broad and unbiased access to services and information, to maintain and preserve materials and equipment, and to continually evaluate the collection to meet the needs of its users. By following these guidelines, school media specialists will be successful in adhering to some of the most important aspects of the professional Code of Ethics adopted by the American Library Association.

Works Cited

American Library Association. (1995). *Code of Ethics of the American Library Association*. Retrieved September 20, 2002, from <http://www.ala.org/alaorg/oif/ethics.html>.

Goehner, D. (1991). "Ethical aspects of the librarian/vendor relationship." In F.W. Lancaster (Ed.). *Ethics and the librarian* (73–82). Urbana-Champaign, IL: University of Illinois.

Selverstone, H. (2001). "Equity of access for all: serving our underserved populations." *Knowledge Quest*, 29(4), 5–6.

Van Orden, P. & Bishop, K. (2001). *The collection program in schools: concepts, practices, and information sources*. (3rd ed.). Englewood, CO: Libraries Unlimited.

Discussion Questions

1. Identify some of your own personal biases or interests that might potentially impact collection selection. How can you ensure that you are making ethical decisions given your own biases?

2. What are some of the ethical decisions you may encounter when making collection selections?

3. What measures can you take to make your collection accessible to all your patrons?

4. What guidelines should you rely on when faced with an ethical challenge as a media specialist?

5. Consider one or two of the scenarios at the beginning of the chapter. Propose appropriate and ethical ways to handle each situation.

Chapter Three
Ethics in School Library Access

By Mary Ann Bell

School librarians are faced with a challenge both old and new: providing equitable access to facilities, resources, materials, and services. Making sure all patrons have access to the library and its resources has long been a key mission of librarians, and today it is complicated by the advent of technology that has brought forth the issue of the digital divide as an additional concern. Studies have shown that school libraries are vital to student achievement, and it is important to ensure that all patrons have the access they need and deserve to both physical and digital resources.

The explosion of technology in recent years has had a profound impact on every aspect of modern life, including public education. Along with many opportunities and advantages, this advent of computer technology presents new dilemmas. One persistent concern has taken the name "digital divide." Barriers to equal access to technology include economic and racial factors, gender, rural versus urban environments, economic environments, and physical disabilities. Sometimes the technology itself may interfere with student access to resources, such as when computerized reading management programs limit students' book choices or when Internet filtering software blocks student access to needed information. The problems of the digital divide have been acknowledged and explored for a number of years, with progress evident in some areas, but the challenges persist. Additionally, as schools do succeed in improving the ratios between computers and students, educators are coming to realize that simple placement of equipment does not solve the problems alone. Indeed, new concerns arise about the quality of equipment, the level of teacher training, and the amount and quality of use of equipment. Thus, the issues of equitable access to the use of technology continue to cause concern for those who wish to include all students in the movement to make the best of technology in schools.

Finally, censorship of materials, whether print or digital, continues to threaten student access to resources. Librarians have the ongoing challenge of seeing that students have access to the best and most varied array of materials possible. Awareness of the need for equitable library access and examination of the issues involved are important for school librarians who wish to provide the best services so that all students and staff can benefit from library use.

Access and Library Scheduling

Much is written about the need for school libraries to be warm, friendly, and welcoming. Librarians strive to create the right atmosphere with displays, promotions, personal contacts, and other efforts. During the school day when the library is open, students need to have ample opportunities to visit. The librarian should make every effort to provide times for individual student visits before school, during lunch, and immediately after school. Librarians should also have reasonable policies in place that welcome students who are sent to the library during class time. Rigid adherence to a fixed schedule for library access can be very limiting to students.

Flexible scheduling has many benefits for providing equitable student access. According to Ohlrich, both flexible access and flexible scheduling offer many advantages to the total school community. By flexible access, Ohlrich means the practice of allowing students to visit the library when needed, easily. They may come to sit and read, to obtain materials, to work at tables, or to receive group instruction. Visitors may be individuals, small groups, or entire classes, with more than one grade level represented at any given time. The atmosphere of such a busy library may result in a higher noise level than that of a rigidly structured environment, but the benefits will be great. Ohlrich describes flexible scheduling as the best way to maximize instructional time and use the library to its best advantage. With flexible scheduling, groups of students or entire classes are planned to take place as needed rather than on a regular rotation. Librarians and teachers work together to develop lessons and plan and schedule work times. Flexible scheduling encourages timely, collaborative lessons and activities. Such lessons can be planned for any available day or time, with the length appropriate for the experience to be provided (2001, 19).

Moving from a fixed to a flexible schedule may seem daunting to administrators, teachers, and even librarians who have not made the change, but those who have switched express a great deal of satisfaction. In Irving, Texas, for example, both librarians and teachers spoke favorably of flexible scheduling. "Despite the initial apprehension, the lessons we all learned about flexible access (scheduling) over the last year have turned most of the skeptics into believers. Teachers and librarians who reluctantly accepted the challenge have openly stated that they cannot imagine going back to a rigid schedule. Many librarians have said this was a most difficult year, but also the most rewarding year of their careers" (Lankford, 1994, 24).

Once flexible scheduling is adopted, the librarian needs to share its successes and advantages in order to ensure its continued use and encourage participation. Publishing facts about library use, news of successful activities, and pictures and stories about library events in school and local newspapers and in formal reports can help focus on the positive benefits of flexible scheduling (Ohlrich, 2001). Whatever situations or constraints face librarians regarding scheduling, librarians must make every effort to provide students with ample opportunities to come to the library during school hours.

Access and Circulation Rules

Flexible access should apply to the numbers and types of materials students can use and take home as well as to the times students can come to the library. One of the best ways librarians can encourage reading and serve avid readers is to have the most generous policies possible regarding the number of items students can check out. A hard and fast rule, limiting students to only one or two items at a time, can keep students from reading for pleasure when research assignments necessitate checkout. Such limits can have a stultifying affect on capable and avid readers who need more materials because they are likely to finish with the allowed number before getting back to the library for additional choices. Also, while it is laudable to encourage students to read at their appropriate levels in order for them to be successful and challenged with the materials they select, there are times when they may be well served with choices that are either much easier or much more difficult than levels identified by standardized tests. An able reader may want an easy choice for pleasure, for the illustrations, because it is something he or she enjoyed in the past and wants to revisit, or for any number of valid reasons. Likewise, a beginning reader may enjoy the illustrations in a difficult book or may be able to read enough to pique his or her interest and imagination. Students may want to take materials home to share with family members or to have parents read to them. As is true with the number of items allowed for checkout, a generous policy regarding levels should be offered.

Additionally, while it is true that in general books are placed in a library reference section based on sound reasons why they should not circulate, the librarian should be open to the idea of allowing references to be checked out when a situation warrants. If a student needs a particular material, regardless of format or location, and there are no compelling reasons to deny access, the librarian should be flexible enough to make an exception. Such a stance is supported by the American Library Association's Library Bill of Rights. In a position paper interpreting the document, it is stated, "The interests of young people, like those of adults, are not limited by subject, theme, or level of sophistication." The document further states that "policies which set minimum age limits for access to videotapes and/or other audiovisual materials and equipment, with or without parental permission, abridge library use for minors," and are therefore unacceptable (ALA, 1991). Keeping in mind that library materials are there for the best possible use by all students, decisions about circulating items in situations that are exceptions to general rules should be made with the students' best interests as the prime consideration.

Access, Library Staffing, and Perception of the Librarian's Role

In order to provide the best services and resources, school libraries must be adequately staffed and funded. Shrinking funds and shifts in the priorities regarding where money should be directed are concerns that can threaten adequate access to school libraries and their resources. Doug Johnson points out that libraries need clerical support staff to handle basic circulation tasks and other routine jobs so that librarians can meet students' and teachers' instructional needs. Schools also need technical support staff that takes care of troubleshooting, installing software and hardware, and keeping up with computer maintenance. Too often, these tasks, clerical- and technology-oriented, fall to the librarian (1999b). This results in reduced opportunities for the librarian to promote reading, to work with teachers, to help students find good books and quality information, to teach information skills lessons, and to do the many other things a professional librarian should do.

One way to promote and protect the library's position as an integral part of the school community is to promote awareness of the library's value. Too often administrators, teachers, and students are not entirely aware of what the librarian does. In a recent *School Library Journal* survey of 242 school principals across the country, this lack of understanding was highlighted. While most administrators believed the school library media center was important, they often had trouble articulating its role. Despite available studies linking strong library programs to student achievement, only 47% said that the two factors were related. Only 27% of respondents reported that their librarians taught classes to students. Over half of the principals said that their librarian's role was primarily that of a caretaker (Lau, 2002b). Mike Eisenberg points out that while it is vitally important to establish and provide an exemplary school library program, it is also necessary to make sure administrators, teachers, parents, and students are aware of what the librarian does and what the library has to offer to them. He proposes an A-B-C approach:

A Articulate a vision and an agenda that define the role of the library and the importance of the teacher librarian.

B Be strategic in planning for success and adopt a positive attitude that breeds successful results. The formation of a library advisory committee can increase patron access to the library decision making process and can broaden the support base for the library.

C Communicate continuously, taking every opportunity to articulate the importance and success of library resources and programs (2002, 47).

Clearly, librarians need to increase communication and work hard to see that their role is understood and appreciated, in order to gain and continue to enjoy the support necessary to provide programs that assure library access.

Access and Economics

Schools and libraries in economically disadvantaged areas face special challenges. Students may lack safe and quiet places to read and work after school hours. They are less likely to have the resources, both print and digital, to conduct research, read for pleasure, or use computers at home. School and community needs are often well served by extended library hours. Extended hours are times that the library is open beyond the regular school day. They may include after the end of the day, during evenings, on weekends, and during the summer. Communities that make the decision to provide necessary funding often do so in hopes of narrowing the achievement gap between students with abundant learning resources at home and those without. The impact of studies such as "The Impact of School Library Media Centers on Academic Achievement," often referred to as the "Colorado Study" (Lance, Welborn, & Hamilton-Pennell, 1993), and other subsequent projects, such as the studies in Pennsylvania, Alaska, and Texas, have resulted in support for extended library hours. Keeping the school library open after regular hours can provide benefits such as:

- Expanding use of the only available library facility for many students
- Increasing student access to computers for research and productivity
- Providing valuable links between the school, homes, and the community
- Engendering good will for the library and school

- Allowing time for special promotions and programs
- Providing opportunities for parents to work with children in the library (Despines, 2001).

Lack of opportunity to use technology among economically disadvantaged students and their families is compounded by the fact that schools in low income areas may have less access and inferior equipment compared to schools in more affluent areas. During the early to middle 1990s, schools were struggling to acquire the equipment needed to meet the growing demands for computers in schools. Once computers were obtained, the next challenge was to bring them online for Internet access. At the same time, more and more families were getting computers for home use, with students in disadvantaged areas falling behind in their access. As John Berry pointed out in June 2002, the problem of disadvantaged homes continuing to lag behind more affluent families in acquiring computers is a continuing and ongoing concern (7).

Some experts optimistically hailed computer access as a way for poorer schools to "catch up" with schools in more affluent areas and expressed hopes that Internet access could make resources more readily available to all. Unfortunately, the cliché of rich getting richer while poor become poorer prevailed in many cases. Schools in less affluent areas still lag behind their counterparts in areas with better financial resources. As reported by Nancy Tumposky, U.S. Department of Commerce figures show that by the year 2000, 84% of schools in districts serving lower income students had Internet access, as opposed to 94% for schools in more wealthy districts. Further, computer use in more affluent areas tended to be more creative and to employ more sophisticated equipment with multimedia capabilities. Computers in the less advantaged settings tended to see more use for routine tasks and drill and practice (2001, 119).

It is certainly true that a number of initiatives have been brought forth to try and address the problem of a gap in computer access due to economic disparity. The Federal E-rate program was highly touted as an antidote and did succeed in helping many schools. Monies were and continue to be available through state and private grants. Many private corporations have helped by providing money through grants and by donating new and used equipment to schools. Public libraries play an especially strong role in helping provide computer access in disadvantaged areas. John W. Berry pointed out in 2002 that 98% of public libraries offered Internet access. He emphasized the commitment of librarians to make technology accessible, particularly in areas where patrons were less likely to have home access (7). School librarians should work with public librarians to encourage student use of all available resources. Still much needs to be done to assure that students in economically disadvantaged areas have continuing and increasing access to needed library resources, both physical and digital.

Access and Race or Ethnicity

School librarians must make determined efforts to provide materials and resources needed by all students, including all members of their populations with regard to race and ethnicity. While English is the historical and customary language of the United States, collections in schools serving communities where other languages are used should offer materials appropriate in language and level to serve all students. Library programs should acknowledge and allow for the linguistic pluralism of their student bodies (AASL, 1990). Furthermore, librarians should celebrate the ethnic and cultural diversity of their schools' communities with programs and displays as well as with materials and resources.

Regarding access to computer resources, special concerns have been voiced about providing access to students of all racial groups. According to John W. Berry, "Americans with low incomes, as well as African Americans and Hispanics, have half the access to the Internet of whites and Asian/Pacific Islanders" (2002, 7). Schools with populations where large numbers of students are likely to be without home computer or Internet access, whether the factors are economic or racial, should make special efforts to meet their students' needs. Circulating laptop computers, providing palmtop devices, opening for extended hours, and other measures can be considered in order to make up for access lacking in homes.

Access in Rural Areas

Students living in rural areas face special challenges to library access. Rural students are less apt to have public libraries available for after school use than their urban counterparts. The combined challenges of rural setting and economic disadvantage result in even less access, both physical and digital, to library resources. Low-income rural homes, especially African-American or Hispanic, are less likely to own telephones and are much less likely to enjoy the benefit of Internet access. This is evidenced by the fact that Black households in rural areas are 40% less likely to have Internet access than the average U.S. Black household. In 1998, rural households lagged behind households across the nation in Internet access by four percentage points. The gap for rural Internet connectivity does seem to be narrowing, though, with rural households reporting access at 38.9% as opposed to the national average of 41.5%, a gain of 2.6 percentage points. The issue continues to be significant in many areas (National Telecommunications, 2001). Rural schools are often community centers, in a very special sense, when other gathering places are limited. As with schools in disadvantaged areas, rural schools can often benefit students and community members by offering extended hours.

Access and Gender

While gender is not usually considered a barrier to physical access to library facilities and resources, it has gained a great deal of attention with regard to digital access. The idea that girls have been less likely than boys to use computers has come to be termed the "gender gap." Numerous studies in recent years have indicated that girls are less adept at using computers and express less positive attitudes toward computer use than boys (Joiner, et al, 1998). Because of their experiences, very young girls are likely to form perceptions:

- that computers are used mainly by boys,
- that computers are often tied to math where boys excel, and
- that computers are machines and they are uncomfortable around them.

An additional deterrent to interest among very young girls is the lack of competent female role models (Bhargava, Kirova-Petrova, & McNair, 1999). In 1998, the American Association of University Women (AAUW) updated its 1992 study of girls and technology. It reported some progress in girls' computer abilities and attitudes but stressed that the gender gap remains a problem. Research also indicates that males and females have different expectations and feelings about computers. While boys enjoy focusing on the technology itself and like to use the computer for its own sake, girls tend to look past the technical aspects of the equipment used and focus on its social aspects of use (Brunner & Bennett, 1997).

"Computers are not culture-free," stated Chisolm. Like all human developments, they carry the beliefs and biases of their creators (1995, 60). Factors contributing to the gender gap may include family attitudes, peer influence, societal perceptions, or curricular and instructional practices (Sanders, Koch, & Urso, 1997). Regardless of cause, the situation needs to be recognized and addressed. Librarians can encourage all students, and girls in particular, to be comfortable and competent users of technology by providing positive and interesting experiences involving technology.

Activities that counteract gender bias build on using technology as a tool, emphasize cooperative and collaborative activities, and present experiences that are motivating and relevant to both girls and boys.

Finally, it should be noted that gender equity is an issue with implications for both girls and boys. Offering activities which appeal only to girls or presenting materials which perpetuate barriers between boys and girls should not be the goal; rather, the goal should be promoting experiences which encourage all students to learn cooperative skills and which all students find engaging and interesting (Furger, 1998). An important first step is to make sure librarians and teachers are aware of the issue. Then, steps to enhance equity include:

- Providing competent role models
- Encouraging activities that are more focused on the computer as a tool for learning, creating, and communicating
- Making sure computers are not promoted exclusively or primarily as "math machines"
- Taking pains to include young girls in activities centered around computer use
- Not allowing class or library computer access to be dominated by a few students who are already proficient and require less guidance and support
- Encouraging social use of computers where students work together on projects

Access and Disability

School library patrons with disabilities have special needs relating to library access. Sometimes the challenges can begin right at library doors. In accordance with the 1990 Americans with Disabilities Act (ADA), entrances and exits must be easily managed with every consideration to access provided for library users. Open areas, reading nooks, displays, and circulation desks should be arranged in such ways as to provide welcoming and accessible use. Many "fixes" may be simple, such as raising tables on wood blocks to allow wheelchair access (ALA ADA, 2000). There must be sufficient space between shelves for wheelchair access and provisions should be considered that allow students to use services such as copy machines, printers, and special display racks. Attention to such details must be ongoing to adjust when needs vary with enrollment changes.

Disabled students can benefit greatly from new technologies but often require adaptations to fit their needs. There are many adaptive options for educators seeking to serve students, ranging from software applications to specific hardware devices. Whether or not to make efforts to meet the needs of disabled students is not an optional topic of concern, it is mandated by law. The Americans with Disabilities Act (ADA) forbids that individuals should suffer discrimination based on disability with regard to employment, programs and services that are provided by state or federal government, and those provided by private and commercial entities (French, 2002). The concepts put forth by ADA have been extended to include cyberspace as well as physical environments. Thus, administrators, librarians, and teachers are constrained to seek out the best methods for serving disabled students in their learning communities.

Library staff members, including aides, volunteers, and student workers, should be trained regarding their service to disabled students and staff. They should be informed of special needs and of ways that they can be of assistance. Workers should be trained to see people with disabilities as individuals who are entitled to full access and who have the same needs and interests as other patrons (Mates, 2002). School librarians should also be leaders, working with administrators and special services personnel, in providing adaptive equipment and resources as needed for students with disabilities. Such additions as large print materials, audio books, Braille devices and resources, and other equipment and resources should be acquired and used as needed.

Librarians also need to remember that consciousness about disabilities extends to patrons with learning disabilities as well as physical challenges. Audrey Gorman defines learning disabilities as disorders "in one or more of the basic processes involved in understanding written or spoken language" and reports that 15% of the U.S. population is affected to some degree (1997, 52). Awareness of the situation is a first step in helping students with learning disabilities. Other measures for helping students with learning disabilities include using multimedia formats in book talks and other presentations, circulating audiotapes, and understanding that a child's actions may be affected by disability rather than simple misbehavior.

Students with disabilities frequently have particular difficulties in their attempts to use computers at school, at public libraries, or at home for online learning. Their efforts are often frustrating, at best, and impossible, at worst. According to the report *Falling Through the Net: Toward Digital Inclusion*, people with disabilities are only half as likely to have Internet access as do individuals without disabilities. The 42.1% access reported by people without disability contrasts with a mere 21.6% for those who are disabled. Certain disabilities, including impaired vision and a lack of manual dexterity, can bring the average even lower. Not surprisingly, the combination of disability and disadvantage due to race or economic means causes even less chance for access for people who fall into these categories (National Telecommunications, 2001).

What are challenges facing those who are making efforts to develop adaptive measures for disabled students in their populations? First, they must take care to provide the necessary means for students to use the technology available to all other children on their campuses. Next, they must make adaptations to any Web-based resources provided for students who need them. Depending upon the nature of their disabilities, students can be well served by a number of adaptive devices that make computer use possible. Many software solutions exist to meet particular needs. Screen-reading software can help individuals with impaired vision. Voice-recognition software helps people who find it difficult to use a keyboard (Vaccarella, 2001). Word processing programs with spell check can be a boon to students with learning disabilities. Programs with features such as built in scanning, easily adapted text size, and speech output can help students with a number of disabilities (Stoddard & Nelson, 2001). Librarians, teachers, and administrators need to be aware of the existence of such adaptive devices and programs and need to actively seek their acquisition.

Not only do disabled students and staff need access to technology in the physical school setting, they also need access in cyberspace. Educators need to be sure that Web based library, academic, and student services are accessible. Again, this is not only the right thing to do but also the law. In 1998, President Clinton signed into law Section 508 of the 1973 Rehabilitation Act. Section 508 states that citizens with disabilities should have comparable access to information that is available to the general public. In other words, people with disabilities should not have less access to materials and resources than other patrons as a result of their conditions. According to an American Library Association Fact Sheet, Section 508 "Requires all federal agencies and certainly federally funded services to make all of their communication and technology accessible," and this includes public and school libraries. The ALA document goes on to point out that many "fixes" are relatively simple to accomplish, that adopting measures to allow such access often helps all patrons, and that the digital divide will not be bridged until people with disabilities are assisted as well as all other patrons (ALA ADA, 2000). Furthermore, Section 508 goes on to say that states getting money under the Technology Act State Program must comply (Van Rooij, 2002). The goal is universal Web accessibility. Barriers to reaching this goal include lack of awareness of the problems and lack of knowledge as to how to design an accessible Web site (French, 2002). An additional challenge is the fact that keeping up with adaptive procedures in Web sites is not a one-time effort. Ongoing steps must be taken to continue enhancing accessibility as the technology for so doing develops and evolves.

During initial Web site development, designers must take care to include the necessary features that can make a page accessible to someone with a disability. In a recent presentation, Cynthia Rowland stressed three reasons for making Web sites available for all:

- It is the right thing to do in that it serves all students equally.
- It is the smart thing to do in that it tends to save money and require cleaner html coding.
- It is the law, referring to legislative measures mandating access for disabled individuals (2002).

Rowland stressed the importance of making pages easily accessible via screen reading software that reads the code and allows a user to move around a Web page. She pointed out that simple adaptations, such as considering color blindness when selecting backgrounds and fonts, are obvious and easy measures to take. Designers must make sure alternative text is available for screen reading software so that it does not skip over illustrations and links. Arrangement of links on a Web site so that it is not necessary to move through the entire page to get to commonly used links is another simple adaptation. Frames in Web pages should be carefully constructed so that they do not delay or interfere with access. There are a number of online helps and print publications to guide Web developers in constructing Web sites that are accessible to disabled users. Designers can test out Web sites using online validation resources that check for universal accessibility and provide feedback about problem areas. Two leading sites in this arena are Bobby™, offered by the Center of Applied Special Technology (Watchfire, 2002–2003), and W3C's html validation service (W3C, 2003), a free resource devoted to this purpose (Rowland, 2002). Technology cannot resolve all problems facing students with disabilities, but it offers a number of opportunities to enhance student learning and brings disabled students into more active participation in learning environments.

Access and Equipment Quality

While it is true that the numbers show improvement in computer access and Internet connectivity in schools and libraries, these numbers do not tend to take into account the age and quality of equipment counted when making the tallies. Gwen Soloman raises concern about "the new inequalities" in computer access. She highlights two areas of concern:

- Quality of equipment, software, and connections; and
- Quality of use of equipment as it relates to what students are doing with technology at school, and how teachers are using technology in their teaching (2002, 18–24).

Computers counted in surveys are often older models lacking adequate memory and speed to successfully run newer applications or to make Internet use feasible. Schools may still lack the necessary infrastructure to provide fast Internet connections. Many schools that started acquiring computers years ago are now faced with the challenges of updating and replacing equipment and of finding ways to use older equipment productively. Newer machines with multimedia capabilities and adequate speed and power are in short supply in some schools whose computer inventories reflect favorable ratios of computers to students but where many older and less powerful computers are abundant. Some schools have turned to thin client technology as a partial solution to the problem but still need new equipment as well. Meanwhile, new resources are being developed, and advances are being made that cause the need for better hardware, software, and connections to become ever-increasingly important.

Access and Quality of Computer Instruction

Even if schools and libraries have computers, Internet access, and software in place, the best possible quality of their use may be lacking. In addition to providing physical access to library resources, librarians and teachers must make sure that students are offered intellectual access. Students need to be able to find information and understand and use what they find. They need to evaluate information and select the best and most authoritative resources for their use. They must have instruction leading to activities and creation of learning products that encourages critical and creative thinking.

Top quality equipment and software has limited value if teachers and librarians are not providing adequate instruction regarding its use. In order for the necessary leadership to emerge, educators themselves must have the necessary training and impetus to adopt best practices in using technology. A recent National Center for Educational Statistics (NCES) survey reports that only 20% of teachers feel adequately prepared to integrate educational technology into their instruction. Again, economics enters as a factor, with schools in disadvantaged areas reporting less spending for teacher training in technology than their more affluent counterparts (Solomon, 2002).

A recent report by the Pew Internet and American Life Project shows that students are acutely aware of the need for quality computer use in schools and the fact that many teachers and librarians are unprepared to provide necessary leadership. Key findings include the reality that many students see their school computer use as far less productive and useful than their home use. While many students report that they use the Internet in numerous ways to work on school assignments, they express frustration regarding use while on campus. Barriers they report include lack of physical access due to limited library or lab hours, interference of Internet filters, and lack of teacher preparedness or willingness to use computers. Even within technology rich schools, access may vary widely, with some teachers employing creative techniques and others barring access entirely. Many teachers are, in students' eyes, hesitant to use technology because they may reveal that they know less than their students. Students who lack computer and Internet access at home express particular frustrations when their attempts to gain access at school are stymied. Students often report that the computer access they have is for rote learning activities or for assignments that fail to use technology in creative, challenging activities. Students call for increased technical support and teacher training so that their school uses of technology may benefit from improved instructional leadership (Levine & Arafeh, 2002).

Librarians are often called upon to be leaders in encouraging quality technology instruction on their campuses. Certainly, librarians need to inform themselves and others about the best informational resources available to their patrons. They should work to encourage combined use of print and digital references. Effective use of informational databases should be demonstrated to teachers and students alike. Librarians need to lead the way in modeling and informing others about the importance of Web site evaluation and successful search strategies. As always, librarians must be leaders in promoting respect for intellectual property. Students who are used to cutting and pasting at will need guidance about avoiding plagiarism and citing sources. The need for librarians to keep up with new developments in educational technology and information retrieval is an ongoing priority.

Access and Computer Based Reading Programs

Technology can certainly enhance students' school experiences. Many approaches that involve computer use report increased student motivation simply because the technology, in and of itself, can be a draw. It is a misnomer, however, to conclude that all technology based activities are superior to experiences not using technology or to assume that computer use to promote reading necessarily has intrinsic benefit in and of itself. One area of technology use in schools that is often debated, and which is of direct interest to librarians as well as to teachers, is the dependence on computer based reading programs such as Advantage Learning's *Accelerated Reader*™ and Scholastic's *Reading Counts*™. In these programs, a student reads a book from a prescribed list and takes a multiple-choice test. Choices of books are limited by reading level, and herein lay problems regarding access. The tests that determine students' reading levels, which are normally given at the beginning of the school year or the outset of a program's implementation, include the *Lexile Framework* used by Scholastic, and Advantage Learning's own system called *Advantage Tossa Learning Standard*. These tests assign each student a reading level based on school grade year followed by a decimal and a number for month, such as 3.7, indicating third grade, seventh month (Chenowith, 2001). In some instances, very narrow ranges based on these levels are prescribed to students to govern their book choices. Thus, a child may be told he or she can read books between 3.5 and 4.0, no "higher" or "lower" titles are permitted. No other factors are considered in ascertaining a student's assigned level or range, called ZPD or "zone of proximal development" by *Accelerated Reader*™. As Biggers notes, the use of this phrase is ironic because it was introduced by Lev Vygotsky, who refuted the idea that testing alone could identify a child's ability. Evaluation based solely on tests, such as those in *Accelerated Reader*™ and *Reading Counts*™, does not take into account the many other factors that work together to determine a student's reading ability, including written responses, extended activities, or repeated interaction with text. Another factor that does not gain much consideration with computerized reading programs and their leveled lists is student interest. As Biggers points out, a student with a high degree of interest in a topic will successfully read more difficult material, while a student with low interest may falter reading easier text (2001, 72–76). Librarians, teachers, and students often express frustration with the levels assigned by computerized reading management programs. Strict adherence to levels causes problems such as blocking a student from reading additional books by an author he or she likes, denying the student the chance to read books in a preferred series, and keeping him or her from enjoying the simple pleasure of browsing library shelves freely. In many schools, the lists of purchased tests heavily favor fiction over nonfiction, causing whole sections of books to be neglected because there are no tests available for them. In some schools, acquisition of books may be greatly influenced by the reading management program, to the exclusion of other material choices. Books whose titles match titles on test disks may be favored over other selections of equal or superior quality. Librarians should base materials selections on quality, instructional value, and student interest. Choices driven by test lists may result in exclusion of other items to which students should have access.

Reading management programs do have supporters who favor their use for tracking, recognizing, and promoting student reading. Doug Johnson points out that when the programs are used for these purposes as part of a larger reading program, they can contribute to a school effort to promote and improve reading. He suggests some guidelines for successful use, including:

- Emphasize personal accomplishment rather than promote competition between students. Recognize groups for progress as well as individuals who excel.
- Make the program one part of a total reading program.
- Allow plenty of chances for students to read for the sake of reading, enjoying books not tested, as well as promoting the reading of books on the test lists.
- Avoid material rewards such as food, or trinkets (1999a).

If the decision is made to use a computerized reading management program, the librarian should become familiar with the best practices regarding its use. Students should have free choices of books to check out and read as well as access to selections from test lists. Providing access to the books children want and need should be a goal of paramount importance.

Access and Censorship

Censorship, as a limiting factor in providing students with access to the materials they need, is a long-standing problem. It continues to take its toll on librarians' and teachers' choices of materials to use and students' abilities to obtain the resources they want and need. In addition to the traditional challenges to books and audiovisual materials, digital resources are also coming under fire. Over the years, librarians, administrators, and teachers have been called upon to defend textbooks, library books, periodicals, videotapes, and myriad other materials available for school use. Today particular pressure is put on schools to limit choices to children's and young adult books, multicultural resources, and materials dealing with topics subject to public, religious, and political debate. Pressure can come from individual parents who feel threatened by children's free access to information or from organized groups who seek to censor based on their particular beliefs. In either case, the results are the same: challenges to materials in all formats (Simmons & Dresang, 2001).

Librarians must continue to be prepared for challenges to materials. They need to have strong and current selection policies and need to be ready to deal with concerned or even irate patrons. The school or district selection policy should guide the librarian in choosing materials that are appropriate for students' levels and interests and that support the school curriculum. Once materials are acquired, the librarian should be prepared to meet challenges that might arise, with the procedures well defined in the selection policy. Librarians should know their collections and be prepared to defend all selections, whether the materials are known to generate concerns or are items not usually known to cause controversy. Again, careful selection is key to the process. Librarians should avoid the pitfall of failing to choose materials that are appropriate but might pose potential problems based on challenges elsewhere or imagined objections from factions in the community. Selection based on anticipated challenges has the same result as removal of materials due to objections.

The librarian should meet objections to materials with calm and professional demeanor. Hearing out a patron who objects to a material in a respectful manner and expressing appreciation for that concern can often result in defusing a difficult situation. Librarians should establish relationships with administrators and decision makers in advance of problems so that if challenges arise, the administrators and decision makers can provide their librarians with necessary support. Administrators and decision makers should be acquainted with the selection policy and should know to use it when challenges or concerns are brought directly to them or when the librarian needs support. Sometimes an administrator fails to follow district policy for review of challenged materials and removes an item personally. In such an instance, the librarian should take the issue to the next level within the district selection policy procedures for addressing challenges to materials. Preparation and resolve to protect student access are needed to protect students' rights to the materials they need.

Access and Internet Filters

Concern about inappropriate Internet content being available on school computers has resulted in voluntary decisions to limit student access to material in cyberspace as well as legal measures to that end. School districts receiving Federal E-rate funding are constrained by law to monitor how their students use the Internet. The Children's Internet Protection Act, or CIPA, requires schools to use computer software that limits access to material that is obscene, pornographic, or otherwise harmful to minors. Further, CIPA states that all districts should adopt Internet safety plans that mandate safe and prudent use of computer technology and electronic communications (Willard, 2002).

The American Library Association has taken a stance opposing the use of filters on the grounds that they deny access to materials students need (ALA, 2002). On May 31, 2002, a Philadelphia court, in a case in which the ALA was one of the litigants, ruled the Children's Internet Protection Act (CIPA) unconstitutional. The opinion rendered by the court held CIPA unconstitutional because filters overblock, thus limiting access to appropriate material, and underblock, allowing illegal or inappropriate material to pass through. As a result of this court ruling, the Federal Communications Commission (FCC) and Library Services Technology Act (LSTA) were enjoined from withholding funds to public libraries that declined to install filters (Lau, 2002a).

The May 2002 ruling did not have any impact on schools and applied only to public libraries. While the logic in this ruling may at some point lead to a reconsideration of the CIPA's mandate to schools, the situation remains at this time that schools are required to filter (Lau, 2002a). In many cases, administrators, teachers, and librarians find filtering an attractive idea for ensuring appropriate student Internet use. However, the problems with filters are such as to call for close examination of the filters' value. As stated in the Philadelphia ruling, filters often overblock. Art Wolinsky suggests that at least 10 sites are blocked inappropriately for every one blocked appropriately. He goes on to stress that, due to the sheer volume of existing sites combined with the number of new ones appearing daily, filtering companies readily admit that inappropriate sites will slip by (2001, 23).

Students express a great deal of frustration with Internet filters at school. A recent Pew study, *The Digital Divide: The Widening Gap Between Internet-Savvy Students and their Schools*, explored student attitudes about computer use on campuses. In describing school Internet use, students voiced frequent complaints that filters keep them from obtaining necessary and appropriate information. In the words of one high school girl, "I was looking up cattle one day, and the message said, 'you can't be here and you have to be off of it.' " Another student reported, "They think you can't handle it, so it hinders your research. I went on the history page one day and typed in this thing about a country … they wouldn't let me see it and it happened four times and got on my nerves so I stopped using the Internet for the project." Many students indicated a lack of desire to even try to use the Internet while at school because of difficulties with filters blocking material. Students without home Internet access were particularly frustrated because their options for getting the materials they needed were further limited (Levine & Arafeh, 2002).

Librarians are often in the front lines regarding computer access and filters. A frequent place where students find themselves blocked from Web sites is in the library while doing research. If the school's filter allows bypass, the librarian should actively pursue gaining and using the rights to access needed sites while also providing appropriate guidance and supervision. Librarians can also help by finding desired information from available resources, such as informational databases and print materials. The students' access to the information they need should be a top priority. Such access should allow students to seek information of personal interest as well as researching for specific assignments. Librarians should encourage district decision makers to allow Web-based e-mail, which is often blocked by filters. Students without a home computer or Internet access have particular needs for access at school, especially the option to have e-mail and to search for non-instructional resources to pursue their personal interests. Such searching should still be supervised, and students should understand that their rights are based on responsible use.

Librarians should speak out for the rights of their students and teachers to have reasonable access to the materials they need in cyberspace. Serving on the campus technology committee is one way to voice the need for reasonable student Internet access. Other venues for promoting student Internet access include faculty meetings, parent-teacher organization meetings, and publications such as newsletters. While supervision is called for regarding online use, it should not be so restrictive as to negate the benefits of Internet access.

Access and the Future

School librarians will always need to be vigilant and proactive in protecting and encouraging access to library facilities, resources, services, and materials. Some areas where access has been threatened are showing improvement, including certain aspects of the digital divide. The recent report from the National Telecommunications and Information Administration entitled *Falling Through the Net: Toward Digital Inclusion* does show that some groups lag behind others, but that disparities are lessening (2001). Rural households are connecting to the Internet at higher rates than households nationwide. African-American and Hispanic households show improving gains in connectivity, and the gender gap has largely disappeared in many environments. The news is not as optimistic for disabled users, who continue to find computer and Internet access challenging (Compaine, [n.d.]). Disparities do continue to exist in all areas of concern, and continuing efforts are needed to increase and protect access to library facilities and resources for all users.

Access to all library resources whether print, audiovisual, or digital continues to be subject to challenges of censorship. Schoolchildren have ongoing needs to have library access freely provided both during the day and after school hours. School librarians must continue striving to provide the best possible library programs and resources, and to make administrators, parents, community members, and students fully aware of the vital importance of the school library media center.

Works Cited

American Association of School Librarians. (1990). *Access to resources and services in the school library media program: an interpretation of the Library Bill of Rights*. Chicago: American Association of School Librarians. Retrieved January 1990 from <http://www.ala.org/aasl/positions/ps_billofrights.html>.

American Library Association. (1991). *Access for children and young people to videotapes and other nonprint formats: an interpretation of the Library Bill of Rights*. Chicago: American Library Association. Retrieved January, 1991 from <http://www.ala.org/alaorg/oif/childrenandyoungpeople.pdf>.

American Library Association. ADA Assembly, Association of Specialized and Cooperative Library Agencies. (2000). *"Facts: why an ALA disability policy? Why now?"* Association of Specialized and Cooperative Library Agencies. Chicago: American Library Association. Retrieved March 6, 2003, from <http://www.ala.org/ascla/access_factsheet.html>.

American Library Association. (2002). *Libraries, the Internet and filtering: ALA fact sheet*. Chicago: American Library Association. Retrieved March 6, 2003, from <http://www.ala.org/alaorg/oif/librariesfact.html>.

Berry, J. W. (2002). *Equity of access: our continuing challenge*. American Libraries. 33(6), 7.

Bhargava, A., Kirova-Petrova, A. & McNair, S. (1999). "Computers, gender bias, and young children." *Information Technology in Childhood Education*. 263–274.

Biggers, D. (2001). "The argument against *Accelerated Reader*™." *Journal of Adolescent and Adult Literacy*. 45 (1), 72–76.

Brunner, C. & Bennett, D. (1997). "Technology and gender: differences in masculine and feminine views." *NASSP Bulletin*. 81(592), 46–51.

Chenowith, K. (2001). "Keeping score." *School Library Journal*. 47 (9), 48–52.

Chisholm, I. (1995). "Equity and diversity in classroom computer use: a case study." *Journal of Computing in Childhood Education.* 6, 59–80.

Compaine, B. M. [n.d.] Epilogue. *The digital divide: facing a crisis or creating a myth?* Compaine (Ed.). Cambridge, MA: MIT Press Sourcebooks. 337–339.

Despines, J. (2001). "Planning for extended hours: a survey of practice." *Knowledge Quest.* 30(2), 22–26.

Eisenberg, M. (2002). "This man wants to change your job." *School Library Journal.* 48 (9), 46–50.

French, D. (2002). *E-accessibility: United States and international.* Proceedings of Ed-Media World Conference on Educational Multimedia, Hypermedia and Telecommunications. Denver, Colorado. June 2002. CD-ROM. Association for the Advancement of Computing in Education.

Furger, R. (1998). *Does Jane compute?* New York: Warner Books.

Gorman, A. (1997). "The 15% solution: libraries and learning disabilities." *American Libraries.* 27(1), 52–53.

Johnson, D. (1999a). "Creating fat kids who don't like to read." *Library Talk.* 12(4), 64.

Johnson, D. (1999b). "Why do librarians need all those support people?" *Knowledge Quest.* 27(4), 43–44.

Joiner, R., et al. (1998). "The effects of gender expectations of success and social comparison on children's performance on a computer-based task." *Educational Psychology.* 18, 319–326.

Lance, K.C., Welborn, L., & Hamilton-Pennell, C. (1993). *The impact of school library media centers on academic achievement.* Castle Rock, CO: Hi Willow Research and Publishing.

Lankford, M. D. (1994). "Flexible access." *School Library Journal.* 40(8), 21–24.

Lau, D. (2002a). "CIPA ruling: no effect on schools." *School Library Journal.* 48(7),16–17.

Lau, D. (2002b). "What does your boss think about you?" *School Library Journal.* 48(9), 52–55.

Levine, D. & Arafeh, S. (2002). *The Digital Disconnect: The Widening Gap Between Internet-Savvy Students and Their Schools.* Washington D.C.: The Pew Internet and American Life Project. Retrieved 2002 from <http://www.pewinternet.org/reports/toc.asp?Report=67>.

Mates, B. T. (2002). *Adaptive technology for the Internet: making electronic resources accessible to all.* Chicago: The American Library Association. Retrieved April 2002 from <http://www.ala.org/editions/samplers/mates>.

McKenzie, J. (1999). "A Brave New World of padlocked libraries and unstaffed schools?" *From Now On: The Educational Technology Journal*. Retrieved February 1999 from <http://www.fno.org/feb99/padlocked.html>.

National Telecommunications and Information Administration. (2001). *Falling through the Net: toward digital inclusion*. Retrieved November 2001 from <http://www.ntia.doc.gov/ntiahome/fttn00/contents00.html>.

Ohlrich, K. (2001). *Making flexible access and flexible scheduling work today*. Englewood, CO: Libraries Unlimited.

Rowland, C. (2002, June). *Making web pages accessible*. Proceedings of Ed-Media World Conference on Educational Multimedia, Hypermedia and Telecommunications. CD-ROM. Denver, Colorado. Association for the Advancement of Computing in Education.

Sanders, J., Koch, J. & Urso, J. (1997). *Gender equity right from the start*. Mahweh, NJ: Lawrence Erlbaum, Associates.

Simmons, J. & Dresang, J. (2001). *School censorship in the 21st century: a guide for teachers and school library media specialists*. Newark, Delaware: International Reading Association.

Solomon, G. (2002). "Digital equity: it's not just about access anymore." *Technology and Learning*. 22(9), 18–20.

Stoddard, S., & Nelson, J. (2001). "Math, computers and the Internet: better employment opportunities for persons with disabilities." *American Rehabilitation*. 26, 9–15.

Tumposky, N. R. (2001). "Technology and Equity in a Democracy." *The Educational Forum*. 65, 119–127.

Vaccarella, B. (2001). Finding our way through the maze of adaptive technology. *Computers in Libraries*. 21(9), 44.

Van Rooij, S. W. (2002). *Making Web-based academic and student services section 508 compliant: whose job is it anyway?* Proceedings of Ed-Media World Conference on Educational Multimedia, Hypermedia and Telecommunications. CD-ROM. Denver, Colorado. Association for the Advancement of Computing in Education.

W3C. (2003). *HyperText Markup Language (HTML) home page*. Retrieved January 16, 2003 from <http://www.w3.org/MarkUp/>.

Watchfire Corporation. (2002-2003). *Bobby™*. Retrieved January 16, 2003 from <http://bobby.watchfire.com/bobby/>.

Willard, N. (2002). Complying with federal law for safe Internet use. *School Administrator*. Retrieved March 6, 2003, from <http://www.aasa.org/publications/sa/2002_04/focWillard.htm>.

Wolinsky, A. (2001). FilterGate. *Multimedia Schools*. 8(3), 22–27.

Discussion Questions

1. In an effort to bring the district up to speed with technology, the technology director of your district has proposed a plan by which new computers will be purchased for the high schools, but the middle schools will get all the current computers in the district and the elementary schools will receive donated machines coming from a local industrial plant. You have heard that the donated machines are out of date and have been poorly maintained. What is your ethical responsibility?

2. Your principal is concerned about security in your high school. After school, all students must vacate the building immediately after the final bell. What access implications will this have, and how will ethical considerations weave into your operational decisions?

3. How do mandated reading program implementation requirements conflict with library ethical positions?

4. Describe a plan to ensure that students without computers or Internet access at home can be assured of equal access to technology.

5. School librarian ethics has a foundation in the first amendment. What steps should you take to ensure that your library provides access to all points of view, including those that may not be politically popular?

6. For a group that may lack access to information, describe the status of the problem, its dimension, and a way that the school librarian may ameliorate the deficiency through the school library program.

Chapter Four
Confidentiality in the School Library

By Harry Willems

Firⁱrst Amendment freedoms are most in danger when the government seeks to control thought or to justify its laws for that impermissible end. The right to think is the beginning of freedom, and speech must be protected from the government because speech is the beginning of thought (Justice Kennedy, Majority decision written on April 17, 2002, 1996 Child Pornography Prevention Act).

Terrorism and the terrorist attack on America have given confidentiality in the public arena a bad name. In the name of patriotism and security, some would give up the time-honored library policy of confidentiality. The librarian's job is tougher now. "It was easier when our only enemies were a few extremists pushing their narrow view of what sexual information people ought to be able to get to in the library" (Berry, 2002, 8). Some of the common breaches of confidentiality in the school library setting are:

- **Non-automated circulation systems that require a signature**
  Signing circulation cards leaves a trail for all to see. Even card systems can use numbers instead of names.
- **Internet sign-up logs**
  If sign-up sheets are used, they need to be destroyed regularly. Besides keeping down the clutter and papers to file, this method protects the confidentiality of persons using the Internet. The ability to connect time and place with a name is a breach of confidentiality.
- **Posting overdue notices with names and titles (or reading names aloud in class)**
  While this method is used to produce group pressure to return books in elementary schools, it is a breach of confidentiality on any level.
- **Concerned discussions about weird reading habits**
  The ethics of librarianship should always be near the consciousness level. When conversations stray into discussions of reading

habits we need to be aware of our responsibilities of protecting confidential information.

- **Indiscreet reference interviews**
  We need to be aware of our surroundings, including other students. Voice level, private space, and notes about conversations of sensitive topics need to be protected.
- **Books with reading levels indicated on the outside cover**
  Reading programs should be administered with confidentiality in mind. Convenience for the library staff should not take place over confidentiality.
- **Automated reports left lying around unattended**
  Certain patron record reports that allow us to find lost materials should be kept out of sight from students, student assistants, and colleagues.
- **Using untrained or poorly trained para-professionals that have not been taught to use written library confidentiality policies**
  Paraprofessionals are the salvation of many a school librarian. They allow the librarian to attend to the administrative and leadership parts of running the library. Paraprofessionals need to be trained in the ethics of librarianship and need to acknowledge that they have read and understand the confidentiality policies of the library.
- **Using untrained student assistants that have access to patron records and reports**
  Student assistants can be of immeasurable help for repetitive tasks. Since they are often left alone in the library, they too need to understand and acknowledge the library confidentiality policy or they should not have access to sensitive reports. In most circulation systems, levels of access can be set by password. Administrative reports should be off-limits to students.
- **Making assumptions about controversial material—how it will be used**
  Materials sought in conjunction with assignments or in normal library activities should not automatically raise red flags. Students who are genuinely hurting or depressed, or students making suicide statements, will cause us to use professional judgment. Be very careful not to confuse the two.
- **Employing software that collects data directly related to student identification, including filtering software, security software, and network software**
  Librarians should be in the vanguard of protecting the confidentiality of students. Effective leaders will provide justifications

and apply ethical standards in the face of opposition and cool technology.

■ **Employing Internet filtering software that reports violations by student ID or time utilized**
"Wet paint, do not touch" is a magnet for fingerprints. So too is using an Internet filter that produces a false sense of security and does not train the values of information access.

■ **Not holding administrators' feet-to-the-fire when a confidentiality policy is in place**
To avoid confrontation with parents, some administrators would assume the responsibility of removing controversial materials and breaching confidentialities, even when library policies are in place. The librarian's leadership is crucial in enforcing the ethical values of librarianship.

■ **Names and pictures associated with students on Web pages**
Parental permission must be given to identify students on Web pages.

Our founding fathers recognized that the worst attack on freedom often comes from within and usually bit-by-bit. Benjamin Franklin (1706–1790), said: "Those who would give up essential Liberty, to purchase a little temporary safety, deserve neither liberty nor safety" (Franklin, Reply of the Pennsylvania Assembly to the governor, November 11, 1755). School librarians are in a position to stand for the ethics stated in the American Association of School Librarians position statement to provide essential confidentiality to all students and staff (AASL, 1999). The ethical responsibilities of librarians, as well as statutes in most states and the District of Columbia, protect the privacy of library users. Confidentiality extends to "information sought or received, and materials consulted, borrowed, acquired, and includes database search records, interlibrary loan records, and other personally identifiable uses of library materials, facilities or services" (AASL, 1999). There are many other people, some with very good reasons, who have been given the responsibility to ferret out criminals and terrorists, who work to make their jobs easier by eliminating the constitutional safeguards of confidentiality. Ann Symons in "Protecting the Right to Read" points to 1970 when bombings brought in the U.S. Treasury agents. She quotes David Berninghausen, chair of ALA's Intellectual Freedom Committee.

When the time comes in any society that government officials seek information as to what people are reading, it must be presumed that they expect to use these records as evidence of dangerous thinking … (Symons, 1995, 14).

School librarians are in the forefront of acting as balance to protect the confidentiality of the students we serve. Beyond that, the chilling effect losing confidentiality would prevent the normal school age person from exercising full advantage of the school library. Carolyn Caywood, Bayside Area librarian, Virginia Beach Public Library, and author of "YA Confidential" says: "Privacy is a particularly acute issue for teens. Adolescence is fraught with worries about peer acceptance and teens suspect that they won't grow up to be the person they imagine. Anything that could expose a teen to ridicule, whether it be taste in reading or ignorance on a subject, looms as a serious threat" (1996, 41). Information access, and the right to keeping our records private, will ensure the relevancy of library service long after graduation. Confidentiality is only one of the facets of the broader topic of intellectual freedoms (IF). Occasionally, insight into several of the other parts of IF can provide context to our topic of confidentiality.

> There are strong winds blowing and some people's matches have gone out. There are thousands of American's cowering in darkness now exactly as their ancestors cowered in feudal Europe. This is a fact that we must face: but I believe there is comfort in facing it squarely and examining carefully the kind of people who have lost their lights. If we look at those lights that are flickering, or going out, and find reasonable explanations for them, we shall know far better where the country stands and what to expect. Those blown out first and most easily are, of course, in exposed positions ... The lights that are flickering now are the lights that have flickered in every great crisis and that will always flicker when stormy winds do blow. However, their flickering has never meant, and does not mean now, that the beacon is about to be extinguished. It will never be extinguished as long as there is a clear, steady flame among the inconspicuous. — Gerald W. Johnson, 1951 (in Jenkins, 1995, xii)

Historical Perspective

The ALA was founded more than a hundred years ago and has since moved from the position of protecting the public from "questionable literature" to defending the public's right to read. Before the "Great War," there were few school librarians, but censorship was noted in the exclusion of several magazines, notably, *Nation* and *The New Republic*. The Library Bill of Rights was passed by ALA in 1939, and 1955 saw the rights extended to children and young adults in the School Library Bill of Rights. Curiously, this document was in response to the McCarthy "witch hunts," rooting out

Communism wherever shadows appeared. Nine years later AASL joined with the NEA's Department of Audiovisual Instruction to ensure standards for school media programs. They stressed the importance of written policies adopted by school administration and boards of education. The turmoil of the 1960s caused concern among some in library schools. They began to "ask basic questions concerning the terrain that the professionals covered and the limitations to intellectual freedom that it may entail" (Samek, 2001, 19). As far back as 1967, David Berninghausen "warned that library school graduates had little knowledge and understanding of key areas of professional concern, such as ... attacks on intellectual freedom, censorship, the ethics of librarianship" (Samek, 2001, 19). Just a year later, Kenneth Kister, Simmons College, agreed with Berninghausen and developed a new course titled: "Intellectual Freedom and Censorship." The point of Kister's course was not to "evangelize for glorious intellectual freedom." Rather, Kister hoped that it would "encourage each student to evolve an individually satisfying, workable, and coherent personal/professional philosophy concerning intellectual freedom, so that as a librarian he will be prepared to make consistent judgments about freedom and censorship questions on the basis of understanding, not fear and ignorance" (Samek, 2001, 19).

Blanket Policy Protection

The Web gives us many examples of protection of the confidentiality of library records, records that directly identify students or patrons. According to the ALA Web site, all states except Hawaii and Kentucky have confidentiality laws, and these two states have attorneys' general opinions on library confidentiality. Several states provide blanket coverage to school libraries; among them are Nebraska statue *84-712-05*, Vermont statute *VSA 317* and Michigan statute *#15.1795* (2,3). Kansas statute *45-221* provides exemption from the open records act but only for public libraries. School libraries are not covered under this statute and are thus do not have statutory protection. Kansas's school records are protected by the provisions of the Federal Educational Rights Privacy Act (FERPA). The Wichita (Kansas) Public Schools Policy 5501 states that pursuant to (FERPA) all student records are private. FERPA has been called into question by the Supreme Court ruling in *Owasso Public Schools vs. Falvo* (2002), which seems to suggest that only the official school records, not all records, may be covered. While the record is still a bit opaque, library records such as circulation, Internet logs, and check-out lists may not be included in this protection. FERPA was passed in 1974 to protect school records from the view of anyone but authorized personnel and parents or guardians of students. In some schools, when enforcement personnel shows up in the school office, principals bend over backward to prevent negative publicity from reaching the local constituents. Library records are easy to sacrifice, and as the controlling authority, the principal may just demand circulation records. So too, when a parent presents a challenge to library materials, the principal may find it expedient to remove materials from the library even if a "challenged-materials" policy is in place. The legal department at the Kansas Department of Education believes the school counselor has the authority to access confidential library information at any sign of troubling behavior (personal telephone conversation with Dr. Jackie Lakin, Information Management Education Program Consultant, Kansas State Department of Education, 2002). FERPA has been amended 25 times since it was passed. "Education records" were defined in the December 31, 1974, amendments as "those records, files, documents, and other materials which contain information directly related to a student; and are maintained by an educational agency or institution" (U.S. Dept. of Ed., 2002). Library records would be covered under this definition. Kent, Washington, school district has a distinct policy (*Policy 4340*) protecting library records, as does Uinta School District #6 in Lyman, Wyoming (Uinta, 2002). Also, the Oyster River High School in Durham, New Hampshire, like so many schools, has a statement of confidentiality in its collection development policy (Oyster, 1997). The Missouri Division of School Improvement provides a confidentiality policy for the state. House Bill *1372 §570.200* identifies "any library of an educational institution" included in the language of the bill. The Missouri *School Library Media Standards Handbook* references the language of the statute, providing the complete text in the "Ethical and Legal Issues" chapter (Missouri, 2002b, 9.16). Some states require that for the protection of library records, the protection granted by the state must be written into a confidentiality statement in library policy. In any event, each library must check with appropriate state agencies to find out how confidentiality laws apply to their situation and the requirements of the legislation. State laws may make library policy easier to write and enforce, or they may only increase the gray areas that media specialists have to deal with.

Confidentiality with Common Sense.

Jan Rice McArthur, in an article in *American Libraries*, confronted an 11-year old student asking questions about suicide. McArthur is a library media specialist at the elementary level in Georgia. As this student opened himself up to her, she found out serious information that needed professional intervention. She confessed to "wondering if he felt that I betrayed his trust ...

the notion of librarian-student confidentiality only momentarily crossed my mind" (McArthur, 1997, 446).

Posing some LM_NET (Library Media e-mail list) questions I found similar sentiment from several school librarians. The questions that I asked were:

1. Who should have access to circulation records?
2. Is a school librarian's duty to confidentiality different from a public librarian's duty?
3. Do we need to sacrifice confidentiality to protect our freedoms?

I also asked for anecdotal information about confidentiality. Several respondents injected intervention stories that prevented tragedies. Robert Hauptman, the staunchest defender of confidentiality, injects:

> ... it [confidentiality] should not be confused with refusal to aid and abet egregiously antisocial acts in the name of some higher obligation. Claiming that patrons [students] may only be interested in reading about something is an easy way to avoid rendering a difficult judgment. Professional disseminators of information must assume responsibility for every action they take; they must make individual decisions based on a complex of principles and necessities and not merely react casuistically because of their training. If they do not think and make adjustments, they have missed the most important aspect of the pedagogical process. It is too easy to confuse education with indoctrination, and a cadre of indoctrinated professionals is oxymoronic (1996, 329).

Privacy: A Basic Human Value

The dignity of the individual is basic to our society. "It defines man's essence as a unique and self-determining human being" (Garoogian, 1991, 218). "Dignity is rooted in religion where privacy is the rational context for love, trust, friendship, respect, and self-respect" (218). Human dignity is dependent on self-determination or personhood. "An individual has a claim to privacy [confidentiality] based on the requirements of self-determination in respect to a person's basic needs" (219). "In the absence of privacy, there are no persons to act as either subjects or agents of moral actions or moral descriptions" (221). As soon as confidentiality is violated, the trust given to us is gone and we stand to do great damage to a person's human needs. Garoogian says:

When faced with decisions regarding request for information of a private nature, librarians may often find themselves involved in the age old conflict between the common good and the sanctity of the individual member of society ... In all cases, whether it be a request from a family member, a law enforcement agent, or a reporter, the librarian is ethically and legally bound to make every effort to protect the individual's right to privacy no matter how convincing the argument for the release of such information appears in the light of the greater good ... A person's independence, dignity, and integrity are violated when one's right to privacy is infringed upon ... Librarians are in a very powerful position since they have direct access to the private reading and subject interests of their users. They have been entrusted with this power. It is therefore, their moral obligation to keep this information confidential (217).

Two Edged Sword

Confidentiality is a two edged sword. The protection against sensitive student circulation information, or even benign information, spreading far and wide in a school setting is only half of the equation. Confidentiality also protects the librarian. The ethics of one's profession are known to a large segment of society. The school librarian will very soon damage his or her reputation by being seen as a "turncoat" or an unethical player if confidentiality is not kept as required by the profession's ethical standards. What would you say to a colleague that says, "Why don't you uphold the ethics of your profession?" Carolyn Caywood also says: "In libraries, confidentiality has as much pragmatic as philosophical support. I don't want to be responsible for vast quantities of data! Once I have information, someone's going to expect me to act on it and that can only get me in trouble. Of course, schools are different from public libraries ... I think schools would have the same practical reasons to be careful" (Caywood, personal e-mail, 2002). We would be hard-pressed to be taken seriously on any other ethical considerations that librarians hold dear. How can we refuse to comply with the question about making "off-air" videos on a timed schedule if we can jettison the ethics of confidentiality? Inconsistency will ruin a librarian's reputation.

To be an effective librarian, one must know when to be the librarian and when to heal the ills of society. They rarely, if ever, happen at the same time. Librarians, in public schools, are supported by taxes from the whole community and they must serve the whole community of students. Reading tastes and personal values vary widely among students. To make lifelong readers we must provide materials for all readers' tastes and must respect the confidentiality of all of students.

Confidentiality Leaks:
Internet Filters and Technology

Internet filters, except when used by parents in the home setting or by businesses to protect productivity, can be ghastly leaks in confidentiality. Out-of-the-box settings on most Internet filters are set to the most restrictive settings possible. Some filters log, by time and address, where the computer has traveled along the Internet. Couple this information with activity logs, sign-in logs, and the trail of any student can be followed right down to the sexuality and STD sites allowed by the filter. For networked libraries, system administrators (sysops) can use the networking software to track the Internet sites visited. Most browsers, Microsoft Internet Explorer™ and Netscape™ for example, have cookie files, history files, "recent" files, and cache files that cache Web addresses. They are logged by time, address, type of file, and so on. If the browser configuration went untouched, or if the network needed no security, the user would be able to delete these files assuming the user were technologically savvy enough to find them all. Security software, such as the death trap "policy editors" to WinnU™ (A Bardon Data System product with security-oriented simplified replacement user interface) and others, can and often do restrict access to files so that the information gathered is only accessible to those with passwords. Methods provided by software applications to clear recent files, cookie files, and caches can be blocked, but that sets up conflict between the need for security and the need for confidentiality. Technology has changed the way we approach confidentiality.

The Children's Online Privacy Protection Act (COPPA) addresses student confidentiality in the use of Web pages. COPPA requires that parental permission be obtained before information is solicited about students under the age of 13. "COPPA appears to have established a situation where such activities are considered OK as long as the site has given parents the opportunity to say 'no' " (Willard, 2002, 6). The Student Privacy Protection Act was included in the No Child Left Behind Act. The U.S. Department of Education is writing the regulations for implementation of this legislation at this moment. The law refers to the collection of information by market research companies. Under the law:

- ■ Schools are required to develop and adopt policies — in conjunction with parents — regarding the following:
  - The collection, disclosure, or use of personal information collected from the students for the purpose of marketing or selling …

- The right of parents to inspect, upon request, any instrument used in the collection of such information.
- Notification must be made annually.
- Offer an opportunity for the parents to opt out of activities involving the collection, disclosure, and use of personal information collected for marketing.
- Provide the dates that such activities are scheduled (Willard, 2002, 8).

"Educators must be able to distinguish between Web sites that have an exclusive educational purpose and sites that are profiling and advertising" (Willard, 2002, 9).

Web pages are the currency of information access, but the identification of students with name/picture association is a serious violation of student privacy. The occasional need to associate a name with academic work or to identify the names and positions of athletic teams, must be preceded by parental permission. Librarians are increasingly authoring their own Web pages. Student privacy must be an integral part the planning process. "People are still struggling to hold onto the right of privacy at the same time that technology seems to be removing many vestiges of this important interest" (Willard, 2002, 18). School districts must provide the rationale for intrusions into the private lives of students. "The basis of this rationale is learning to distinguish when and where we can and should expect privacy and when and where we should not expect privacy — and then to govern our behavior and communications based on that expectation" (Willard, 2002, 18).

Confidentiality by Degree

Applied Digital Solutions of Palm Beach, Florida, now produces an identity chip to be inserted under one's skin. The chip can be encoded with GPS (global positioning system) information to track the locations of people anywhere with this technology embedded in their skin (Applied, [n.d.]). This is just a small step forward from getting a child's picture and fingerprints and is done to prevent kidnapping or getting lost. This breach of confidentiality that seemed so remote now resembles the "mark of the beast" to some librarians. In a school library setting, one would just have to wave the bar-wand or scanner over the students arm and have all the personal information available to get overdue books back and to even track the kid to other schools in search of lost materials. When does the loss of confidentiality go too far? We can make a case for the "slippery slope" model that seems to indicate that librarians, both school and public, stand on the front lines to protect liberty through protecting confidentiality. Do we need to sacrifice our confidentiality to protect freedom? One who answered my LM_NET post indicated that to give up our rights is to already have given up our freedoms.

The Patriot Act of 2001 (The full title is: *Uniting and Strengthening America by Providing Appropriate Tools Required to Intercept and Obstruct Terrorism Act*) appeals to the best and worst in all of us. Who does not want to be patriotic? Mary Minow, library law consultant with <www.librarylaw.com> confirms that libraries will be affected by the Patriot Act (2002). Similar to the 1970s incursion into libraries by the FBI to thwart bombings, the Patriot Act will intensify the scrutiny of libraries and librarians to see if they're "for us or against us." The three areas covered by the act are:

1. changes in immigration laws.
2. tightened controls on money laundering.
3. greatly expanded the use of electronic surveillance.

The basic issue for libraries is that act requires more surveillance orders on technology, such as installing CARNIVORE software, which gathers and records all Internet traffic. In addition, the Act allows federal agents to get court orders for business records. What are business records? "The production of any tangible things, (including books, records, papers, documents and other items) for an investigation to protect against international terrorism or clandestine intelligence activities ..." (Patriot Act, Title II §215). Test cases have not established precedent for the library at this point. The library should cooperate with security agencies that produce a valid court order (one cannot disclose the existence of the order to anyone, even the target of the investigation). For the student population, the Act is aimed at higher education but has no particular limitations to that. Records that were once collected about students and that were protected by strict privacy provisions, now no longer have those protections (ACLU, 2001, 5). By far the greatest effect of the Act on libraries is the intimidation factor. Librarians are not required to "finger" suspected terrorists, but moral grounds and basic common sense require us to report wanted fugitives and people identified from pictures as wanted suspects. Confidentiality must not be breached by the reading inclinations of patrons, off the cuff banter by librarians, fears of ethnic profiling, or indiscrete reference interviews. In practical terms, school librarians are required to breech any confidentiality associated with individual students at the request of federal officials presenting a court order.

Gary Hartzell also finds that the school principal is not necessarily a paragon of intellectual freedom. Very few, if any, administrative training

programs discuss any of the intellectual freedom issues that are so important for school librarians. In fact, intellectual freedom issues, including
confidentiality, are the legal pitfalls that school administrators see as
pressing problems — problems that could end their employment. A survey
conducted in 1996 surveyed 250 programs and found that only 18% even
talked about the school library. Moreover, out of those, only six of the
professors interviewed actually integrated the subject of libraries (Wilson,
1998, 2). Administrators have many conflicting and competing demands that
must be woven together to provide a smooth running operation. Because the
intellectual freedom issues of confidentiality, copyright, and collection
development are of secondary importance to running a smooth operation,
administrators may be hostile to these ideas. Minus the understanding and
support of the school administration, some school librarians feel validated
that intellectual freedom issues need not be her or his concern. It is hard to
stand up to the administration, and this lack of support or even overt pressure from the administration, shifts the librarian's focus from teaching students to what is considered political maneuvering. The excuse of "I don't
have time for politics" provides the cover to do nothing.

Julie Walker, Executive Director of AASL/YALSA also points to
another issue for school media specialists. The advocacy continuum, from
parent to librarian, may present internal conflicts. If the librarian has not
had a strong grounding in intellectual freedom, his or her own parenting
instincts may, in fact, win out over the ethical responsibility of librarianship
(Walker, personal communication, 2002).

The Invisible Librarian

Without influence, the school librarian is doomed to the ethical standards now
in place. Gary Hartzell does a great job explaining that librarians are invisible
because of external and self-imposed factors. The external factors are discussed earlier in this chapter. The self-imposed factors are ones of acceptance
of our lot. Mr. Hartzell lists four factors in self-created invisibility:

1. Perpetuating the image of a non-educator — something less than
   a professional.
2. Accepting the role of the school library as one of auxiliary or
   fringe service.
3. Maintaining isolation instead of integration.
4. Failing to get involved in the education of students (Hartzell,
   1994, 13).

Without influence, it will be very difficult to be effective advocates for confidentiality and intellectual freedom. Building influence requires that librarians collaborate with faculty and administration, become proficient in technologies and applying curriculum standards, and become leaders in the media center, not being satisfied with only doing the clerical duties.

Prayer Requests: Just Another Way to Gossip?

As a youngster, I remember Wednesday meetings at church where concerns for the congregation were offered as prayer requests. The standard joke became that this was an "acceptable way to gossip." In an editorial in *School Library Journal*, we find a parallel in schools where one needs only to act concerned. Off-hand remarks to colleagues, parents, and administration about the reading habits of students, just to make conversation or worse, to chime in concerns being discussed about that certain student, are serious breaches in confidentiality. Lillian Gerhardt says that librarians often spill their guts "or trade survival information on those who exhibit odd-to-weird tastes in their reading or research interests. It is a fact that we tell each other quite readily what a badge-bearing snoop would have to pry out of us with a warrant" (Gerhardt, 1990, 4). Greenberg and Levy give us a definition of confidentiality that distinguishes sharing legitimate information from breaching confidentiality: "A confidentiality provision is not a blanket pro-hibition against service providers and school staff talking together to coordi-nate services. It is simply a protection against sharing information about a person over that person's objection or sharing information that does not serve a specific purpose that is in a child's or family's interest" (Greenberg & Levy, 1992, 6).

Prisoners Have Rights

Incarceration removes a great deal of the confidentiality that one enjoyed as a free person. It seems that the privilege of schooling is akin to benign imprisonment in which the laws of privacy are suspended. The rights of children and young adults are breached, usually, with the consent of parents. The school, in place of parents (*in loco parentis*), suspends the child's right to confidentiality as situations dictate. There are no limitations on constitu-tional rights in this country, but there is a certain balance between the rights of parents, the school, and the child that often times gets blended into discretionary authority exercised by parents and the school. The rights of privacy are sacrificed to the gods of expediency and legitimate concerns.

Most children, being children, many times just accept the invasions of their rights. For order and control, there does need to be authority structure that assures learning and safety, and this might be a legitimate trade off. In this charged atmosphere, the librarian is a bulwark of intellectual freedom whose voice needs to be heard above the din of the conversation about "homeland security" and Internet filtering.

As librarians, we see the reference interview as a tool to provide good service to students. We need to know why and in what format they need the information to determine how best to provide this service. Some of this information may be too high a price to pay for the student who is seeking sensitive information about parental abuse or sexuality. Even though students may be part of a "captive audience," we as professionals need to keep the concepts of confidentiality in the forefront of everything we do for our captive patrons.

Information access is the correct topic of library instruction today. One of the components of information access is learning about how information is used as power. Alvin Toffler indicates that the three pillars of power are "wealth," "force," and "information" (Toffler, 1990, 15–16). Because information is so critical to society, teaching today's crop of students to be critical and skeptical about the abuses of information, including confidentiality of information, is paramount.

Marketing: The Value of a Good Offense

In public libraries, the absence of marketing the accomplishments in programming, circulation statistics, and services, often results in the library becoming irrelevant to the community it serves. The out-of-sight, out-of-mind mentality dooms the public library to the slippery slope of lack of proper funding and the resulting lack of staffing, new materials, and so on to oblivion. Perception is the key to marketing. It is not how good you actually are, it's how good you are perceived to be that is the key to success.

We have already determined that in the school library an influential librarian has a good likelihood of defending confidentiality and intellectual freedom. One of the most overlooked aspects of "who to influence" in the school setting is the general public. The school librarian must position himself or herself in the community as a resource for parents, grandparents, and the business community. In small communities (where the most IF challenges occur), the librarian must become visible and influential. Influential does not necessarily mean political, however, it may mean covertly political. The librarian's expertise in curriculum, curriculum integration, collaboration, and technical prowess should be showcased at every opportunity.

Finding form and filling out forms of all kinds for parents and senior citizens can be a service to the community that engenders social capital-good will. The school librarian should be in the forefront of literacy programs in the community. Anthony Tilke at the IFLA (International Federation of Library Associations and Institutions) Conference in Bangkok, Thailand, says: "School librarians are remarkably similar to … [librarians in] other types of organizations, such as business, research bodies and hospitals, in as much as they must connect with their customers or user base." In the school setting, the library may be subtly different from other areas of the school. "It is not a classroom, but can be a refuge, a resource bank, a shop-window, an exhibition and display area, a place to 'chill' out, to meet others and relax in" (Tilke, 1999, 3). Marketing the library to students cannot be successful in an atmosphere of censorship and mistrust.

Policy Implications

Many examples of school library policies can be found on the World Wide Web. Policies concerning confidentiality are included in one of several sections. Most likely, the policy concerning confidentiality is included with intellectual freedom issues, such as copyright or book challenges, but also may be found in the mission and philosophy of the library. Sadly, many published policies do not contain references to confidentiality. A simple IF policy would simply state the AASL policy. A confidentiality policy might also contain reference to state laws that give privacy protection to the library and it should affirm the methods used by local and state authorities to gain access to a student's confidential circulation records or other records that directly identify the student. The Missouri State Department of Elementary and Secondary Education provides language in a state policy on confidentiality. We do not need to invent a policy that is already provided for us (Missouri, 2002b). The "Guidelines for Writing a Confidentiality Policy" can be found in Appendix H of that document, along with the full 43-page belief statement (Missouri, 2002a, 18).

This process should not just grow. One should have a plan to write, disseminate draft proposals, gain approval, and disseminate the final confidentiality policy to faculty staff and administration. The confidentiality component of library policy might be easier to insert in a new policy over adding it to an existing one. If the library is without any policies, a confidentiality section must be part of an overall intellectual freedom statement that can be part of, or separate from, a collection development policy. Writing the policy drafts can be guided by the media specialist or librarian or can be written using various templates. One would experience better buy-in support if a committee of faculty were used to help with the process. Above all, keep the administration, including the board of education, appraised of the progress of writing the document. Neither is fond of surprises. Finally, the policy must have the official stamp of the school board. Nothing holds the future administrations' feet-to-the-fire like a board-approved policy.

Conclusion

Today's society places conflicting and sometimes unreasonable demands on the concept of confidentiality. School librarians are in a controlled culture, especially in elementary grades, that opens even library records to the hearing of others. The practice is common for an elementary teacher to read the names of kids with overdue books and probably titles as well, to the whole class. Parties and prizes are given based on everyone conforming to the library overdue policy. Goodies for books returned on time, parties for good library behavior all contribute to the atmosphere and culture of elementary schools. *Accelerated Reader*™ is used in some schools, and to make the program easier to use, the administrator uses different colored labels for reading levels. Librarians who would not otherwise violate a student's confidence are doing just that by having the students carry a sign on every library book saying "I'm a poor reader." Because of the tragedies perpetrated to and in schools, all faculty are encouraged to report suspicious papers, behaviors, and habits of students. Especially at the secondary level, but to a lesser extent at the elementary level, school librarians need to know the reason for policies about confidentiality and work to get the confidentiality message to administration and boards. This does not mean that we cast adrift the concerns of parents and society, but that we are the bridgehead in the loss of freedoms and rights. Ethical standards of our profession demand that we understand and promote confidentiality.

The great achievements of the American society are built on our abilities to find and use information. Confidentiality is paramount in business and business dealings. Our country's current President calls confidentiality essential for getting the best and most accurate information about the nation's pressing issues. And so it is. Totalitarian societies could not and do not flourish without breaching the confidentiality of its citizens. The network of spies in the defunct Soviet society included family members and colleagues. Looking over one's shoulder became an everyday fact of life. Never knowing who was blowing the whistle to put you in jail proved a powerful way to keep the populace in line. In a recent editorial, John Berry addresses the current rush to curtail freedoms:

Yet librarians have the job of delivering access to information, even without strong allies or huge popular support. We can't simply allow government to decide limits of access, nor politicians to legislate away our rights in a flurry of patriotic rhetoric. While we respect legitimate national security concerns, we must quietly resist the extreme application of the new secrecy. We must fight to help the people get the information they need. After all, in a democracy like ours, the people will decide the fundamental questions 'either ignorantly or wisely' (2002, 8).

Works Cited

American Civil Liberties Union. (2001). *USA Patriot Act boosts government power while cutting back on traditional checks and balances.* ACLU Legislative Analysis. Retrieved 2001 from <http://www.aclu.org/congress/l110101a.html>.

American Association of School Librarians. (1999). *AASL position statement on the confidentiality of library records.* Retrieved March 2002 from <http://www.ala.org/aasl/positions/ps_libraryrecords.html>.

American Library Association. (2001). *Privacy resources for librarians, library users, and families.* Retrieved December 2001 from <http://www.ala.org/alaorg/oif/privacyresources.html>.

American Library Association. Office for Intellectual Freedom. (1996). *Intellectual freedom manual.* Chicago: American Library Association.

Applied Digital Solutions. [n.d.] *VeriChip Corporation.* Retrieved March 6, 2003, from <http://www.adsx.com/prodservpart/verichip.html>.

Berry, J. N. (2002). "It was easier to fight a few narrow-minded extremists 'Either ignorantly or wisely' " *Library Journal.* 127(5), 8.

Caywood, C. (1996). "YA confidential." *School Library Journal.* 42(8), 41.

Garoogian, R. (1991). "Library/patron confidentiality: an ethical challenge." *Library Trends.* 40, 216–233.

Gerhardt, L. N. (1990). "Ethical back talk: III." *School Library Journal.* 36(6), 4.

Greenberg, M., & Levy, J. (1992). *Confidentiality and collaboration: information sharing in interagency efforts.* Denver, CO: Education Commission of the States Distribution Center.

Hartzell, G. (1994). *Building influence for the school librarian.* Worthington, Ohio: Linworth.

Hauptman, R. (1996). "Professional responsibility reconsidered." *RQ.* 35(3), 327–29.

Jenkins, C. A. (1995). *The strength of the inconspicuous: youth services librarians, the American Library Association, and intellectual freedom for the young, 1939-1955*. Unpublished doctoral dissertation, University of Wisconsin, Madison.

McArthur, J. R. (1997). "When an 11-year-old wants to take his own life." *American Libraries*. 28(11), 45–46.

Minow, M. (2002). *The USA Patriot Act and patron privacy on library Internet terminals*. Retrieved March 6, 2003, from <http://www.llrx.com/features/usapatriotact.htm>.

Missouri State Department of Elementary and Secondary Education. (2002a). *Belief statement: instructional media center/school libraries*. Retrieved February 2002 from <http://www.dese.state.mo.us/divimprove/curriculum/library/appendixH.pdf>.

Missouri State Department of Elementary and Secondary Education. (2002b). *Chapter 9: ethical and legal issues*. Retrieved February 2002 from <http://www.dese.state.mo.us/divimprove/curriculum/library/chapter_9.pdf/>.

Oyster River High School. (1997). *Library Media Collection Development Policy*." Retrieved March 6, 2003, from <http://www.orcsd.org/hs/library/bdpolicy.htm>.

Owasso Independent School District No. 1-001 a.k.a. Owasso Public Schools, et al. v. Falvo. 2002.

Samek, T. (2001). "Introducing intellectual freedom courses into the Canadian LIS curriculum." *Counterpoise*. 5(1), 19–21.

Symons, A. K. (1995). *Protecting the Right to Read*. N. Y.: Neal-Schuman.

Tilke, A. (1999, August). *The role of the school librarian in providing conditions for discovery and personal growth in the school library. How will the school library fulfill this purpose in the next century?* Conference Proceedings of 65th IFLA council and General Conference. Bangkok, Thailand.

Toffler, A. (1990). *Powershift: knowledge, wealth, and violence at the edge of the 21st century*. New York: Bantam.

Uinta County School District #6. (2002). *"Confidentiality of Library Records."* Retrieved March 6, 2003, from <http://www.uinta6.k12.wy.us/WWW/Admin/%20PolicyManual/Section%20I/IIAD>.

U.S. Department of Education. Family Policy Compliance Office. (2002). *Legislative History of Major FERPA Provisions*. Retrieved on March 6, 2003, from <http://www.ed.gov/offices/OM/fpco/ferpa/leg_history.html>.

USA Patriot Act. H.R. 3162. Title II §215. Amending the Foreign
   Intelligence Surveillance Act (FISA) Title V §501(a)(1). Retrieved
   March 6, 2003, from <http://leahy.senate.gov/press/200110/USA.pdf>.
Wichita Public Schools; Board of Education Policies. P5501, Privacy of
   Pupil Records. <http://www.usd259.com/policies/5501.html>.
Willard, N. (2002). *Safe and responsible use of the Internet: a guide for edu-
   cators*. Eugene, Oregon: Responsible Netizen Institute.
Wilson, P. (1998). "In the dark: what's keeping principals from understand-
   ing libraries?" *School Library Journal*. 44(9), 114–116.

Discussion Questions

1. In a question of confidentiality, discuss the reasons that a librarian would want to support nondisclosure of a patron's personal
   information. How might that position conflict with the position
   of a teacher, an administrator, or a parent?

2. Certain laws will conflict with a librarian's ethical responsibilities. As a rule of thumb, when should a librarian violate a
   patron's right to privacy? Justify your answer.

3. What common library practices routinely violate patron confidentiality? What adjustments can be made to modify these practices to align them with commonly accepted ethical principles?

4. Should certain topics be completely off limits in the school
   library to simplify the problem the librarian has of deciding if
   an information request is appropriate or inappropriate? What are
   the ramifications, both political and operational, of each
   answer?

5. What role, if any, should a librarian's personal beliefs play in
   decisions about confidentiality?

Chapter Five

Ethics in the Use of Technology

By Doug Johnson

At a recent workshop on technology ethics for students, I was (to put it mildly) surprised when one of the thoughtful, lively school librarians attending revealed that she did not realize that one should not publicly post lists that linked student names and titles of overdue materials. It seemed to me to be an issue that was, as our students put it, a "no-brainer" — librarians have an ethical duty to protect the privacy of their patrons. But apparently it is not.

Just how do school library media specialists learn about the ethics of their own professional practice? Sometime during my library school days, I am sure I was introduced to this issue, I learned what I needed to know for the test, and promptly forgot its existence. Administrators for whom I worked have never seemed to scrutinize closely my professional ethics as a librarian.

Had it not been for a series of editorials by Lillian Gerhardt that appeared in *School Library Journal* (1990, 1991), I don't think that I would have remembered that there is a code of ethics for librarians. In these short pieces, Gerhardt interpreted the Code of Ethics of the American Library Association (ALA) in its application to the practice of school librarianship and service to children (as well as shaming the ALA into revising the code). This business of right and wrong was clarified, and she asked me to think about these issues in my daily work. Thank you, Ms. Gerhardt.

The sweeping impact that information technologies have had on school library media programs suggests that we take some time as a profession to look at the ALA's Code of Ethics yet again. We have accepted as part of our mission and charge the ethical education of our students and, to some degree, our fellow educators and parents. However, in order for us to do this with understanding and without hypocrisy, we need to look at the ethics of our own professional practice as it relates to use of information technologies.

While it is impossible to visit every ethical issue that technology touches, I have tried to comment on those that are the most significant or most confusing for the practitioner. We need a continuing dialog in our profession about our own ethical practices. Perhaps this reexamination of the ALA's Code of Ethics is a beginning. See the complete document of the ALA's Code of Ethics in the Appendix.

ALA Library Code of Ethics Statement I

ALA Library Code of Ethics Statement I: *We provide the highest level of service to all library users through appropriate and usefully organized resources; equitable service policies; equitable access; and accurate, unbiased, and courteous responses to all requests.*

Information technologies — computers, the automated catalog, electronic databases, and access to the Internet — have allowed even the most humble school library to offer services even research libraries could only dream of only a few years ago. However, our jobs have become increasingly complex as a result. As Gerhardt suggests in her comments about this statement, it should go without saying that the ethical, or just plain competent, librarian should provide the highest level of service. Let's look at each of these qualities of service in turn to see what issues are emerging because of new technologies.

Resources

School budgeting is a "zero sum" game: there is a finite, and usually inadequate, number of dollars that can be spent by a school district in any one year on the total educational program, including class size, basketballs, toilet paper, staff development, and superintendent's transportation allowance. What this means is that every dollar spent on technology or library resources is a dollar that cannot be spent for other potentially worthwhile purposes. Ethically, we must spend every dollar in ways that will do the most good for our staff and students, keeping the entire school funding picture in perspective.

As informational resources, both print and digital, become available, we need to carefully appraise which format best suits curricular purposes and our budgets. Collection development strategies are more important than ever as our scarce resources need to be stretched to cover ever-higher demands. Materials purchased "just in case" or for a "well-rounded collection" that remain untouched by human hands are not just unwisely, but unethically, acquired.

It is ethically irresponsible *not* to have a budget. Too often, we confuse having a budget with having a fully funded budget. Every library needs to have a written, goal-oriented, specific proposed budget. If students are to have access to the resources necessary for an effective educational program, all school library media specialists must accurately inform decision makers of the cost of those resources. The greater outlays necessary for technology in schools, among other things, makes this more critical than ever.

Policies

The use and abuse of technology resources requires that the school library media specialist must be able to create good policies and rules related to use. While we are rightfully expected to enforce board-adopted policies, such as the Acceptable Use Policy, each individual library has its own set of expected rules and consequences for infractions that are set by the school library media specialist and library committee.

Since technology is a more or less unfamiliar resource for many adults, our policies tend to be overly harsh in proportion to the importance of the act committed. I too often hear a student losing "Internet privileges" for an entire year or semester for a minor or first infraction of a rule. When formulating consequences for rule or policy infractions, school library media specialists need to:

1. Examine the existing consequences for other similar improper activities. If a student sends a harassing e-mail, for example, the consequences for harassment already in place should apply.
2. Graduate the penalties. Students should not be denied access to the Internet for an extended period for a first infraction of the rules. One might ask, "Should a child be banned from reading if he or she were caught reading something inappropriate?" If the inappropriate behavior repeats itself, the penalties can be increased.
3. Bring parents in on any ethical use violation.
4. Allow and encourage student personal use of the Internet. If the Internetworked computers are not being used for curricular purposes, students should be allowed to research topics of personal interest (that are not dangerous or pornographic, of course), chat, or send e-mail to friends. One reason for allowing this activity is that students are far less likely to risk loss of Internet privileges if it means losing access to things that they enjoy.
5. Make sure all rules are clearly stated, available, taught as part of library orientation, and consistently enforced.
6. Develop school-wide ownership of the rules. Having a site-based leadership team or library committee that helps set the rules of technology for a school keeps the librarian from having to be the "heavy" and results in rules that more accurately reflect the culture of the school.

Access

The school library media specialist has an ethical duty to advocate that all students in a school have liberal access to electronic resources. Home access and public library access to information technologies alone will not close the "digital divide." This means serving on building technology teams and advocating for:

1. *Access to technology for all students.* Too often technologies have been acquired and sequestered by certain departments, grade levels, or individual teachers within schools. School library media specialists need voice the need for non-departmental (library) access to information technologies that are available before, during, and after school hours. Our "whole-school" view puts us in a unique position of knowing which children are getting technology skills and access in our buildings.

   Adaptive technologies have made more resources available to the physically challenged than ever before. The school library media specialist needs to be the voice for awareness and adoption of such technologies. We also need to help schools understand and comply with Americans with Disabilities Act (ADA) regulations such as the mandate that all school Web pages be machine-readable by providing alternate text descriptions of all visuals.

2. *The least restrictive use of information technologies.* The pursuit of information by students to meet personal needs should be encouraged in schools. Lifelong learning strategies, practice in information evaluation, and experiences in building effective communication strategies are all reinforced when students use information technologies to meet personal goals.

   As library media specialists and technologists, we need to lighten up a little concerning what students are doing with the Internet in our libraries and classrooms. The Internet has vast resources that are not directly related to the curriculum but are of high interest to students at all grade levels. Information about sports, fashion, movies, games, celebrities, and music in bright and exciting formats abounds.

   The use of the Internet for class work must be given priority, of course, but computer terminals should never sit empty. There are some very good reasons to allow students personal use of the Internet:
   - It gives kids a chance to practice skills. After all that's why we have "recreational" reading materials in our libraries. Do we really subscribe to *Hot Rod* or *Seventeen* because they are used for research? If we want kids who can do an effective Internet search, read fluently, and love to learn, does it make much difference if they are learning by finding and reading Web pages on the Civil War or by playing Civil War games?

- It gives weight to the penalty of having Internet access taken away. The penalty for misuse of the Internet is often a suspension of Internet use privileges. As a student, if I were restricted to only schoolwork uses of the Internet and had my Internet rights revoked, I'd pretty much say "So what?" and would wonder what I had to do to get my textbooks taken away as well. However, if I were accustomed to using the Internet each morning before school to check on how my favorite sports team was faring, the loss of Internet access as a consequence of misbehavior would be far more serious.
- It makes the library media center a place kids want to be. Many of our students love the library for the simple reason that it is often the only place that allows them to read books of personal interest, to work on projects that are meaningful, and to explore interests that fall outside the curriculum in an atmosphere of relative freedom. Kids need a place like that, and we should provide it—even at the Internet terminals.

3. *The greatest range of electronic resources.* E-mail, chat rooms, and instant messages are often banned by schools, fearing their misuse by students. Yet, such resources can put learners in touch with one of the best primary resources — the human expert. The ability to access sound and video files and computer programs is also often banned, even when there is demonstrated instructional need.

Accurate, Unbiased, and Courteous Responses to All Requests

One of my favorite *Calvin and Hobbes* cartoons has Calvin on the phone asking if the library has any books on "why girls are so weird." Frustrated when his need goes unmet, he concludes: "I'll bet the library just doesn't want anyone to know." For some requests, it is genuinely difficult to give an "accurate, unbiased and courteous" response.

Anyone who has worked with children and young adults knows that they probably have as wide a range of interests and information needs as adults. While giving priority to requests for help to meet academic needs, we need to honor all information requests, keeping in mind that we do have a responsibility for providing guidance to our young charges as well. Personal interests can motivate reluctant readers to read, reluctant technology users to use the Internet, and library-shy students to use our resources.

Moreover, I sincerely hope we never forget that *courtesy* is a part of our ethical code. Opinions about libraries and librarians are formed at a young age and are often lifelong. The kids we serve today will be our school board members and legislators of tomorrow.

ALA Library Code of Ethics Statement II

ALA Library Code of Ethics Statement II: *We uphold the principles of intellectual freedom and resist all efforts to censor library resources.*

Technology has opened floodgates of information into schools, primarily by way of the Internet. Along with marvelous resources on topics of curricular and personal interest, the flotsam and sewage of the Internet has become readily available as well. Materials and ideas that had been in the past physically inaccessible to students now can be viewed at the click of mouse button.

The potential for student access to unsavory and possibly unsafe materials on the Internet has made the support of intellectual freedom both more challenging *and* more important. It is difficult to justify a resource that allows the accidental viewing of graphic sexual acts by second graders searching for information on "beavers" or communications by an anorexic teen with fellow anorexics, who encourage the continuation of the disorder. Defending unfiltered Internet access seems quite different from defending *The Catcher in Rye.*

Yet the concept of intellectual freedom as expressed in both ALA's Library Bill of Rights <www.ala.org/work/freedom/lbr.html> and Freedom to Read <www.ala.org/alaorg/oif/freeread.html> statements is as relevant to information in electronic formats as it is in print:

> We trust Americans to recognize propaganda and misinformation, and to make their own decisions about what they read and believe. We do not believe they need the help of censors to assist them in this task.

As expressed in "Access to Resources and Services in the School Library Media Program, an Interpretation of the Library Bill of Rights" <www.ala.org/alaorg/oif/accmedia.html>:

> Although the educational level and program of the school necessarily shapes the resources and services of a school library media program, the principles of the Library Bill of Rights apply equally to all libraries, including school library media programs.

While one must recognize that preventing access to pornographic or unsafe materials is the reason given by those who advocate restricted access to the Internet in schools, there are political motivations behind such attempts to require blocking and monitoring software as well. The fight for intellectual freedom in schools is more important today than ever.

To a degree, CIPA (the Children's Internet Protection Act) has taken the decision to use or not use Internet filters out of the hands of local decision makers. Districts who receive federal funding, including E-rate telecommunications discounts, must install and use an Internet filtering device or other technological measures to be in compliance. Yet, a strong commitment to intellectual freedom on the part of the school library media specialist is possible even in a filtered environment.

Internet filtering can have a wide range of restrictiveness. Depending on the product, the product's settings, and the ability to override the filter to permit access to individual sites, filters can either block a high percentage of the Internet resources (specific Web sites, e-mail, or chat rooms) or a relatively small number of sites. In our role as proponents of intellectual freedom, we need to advocate strongly for the least restrictive settings and generous use of override lists in our Internet filters. We need to make sure that at least one completely unblocked machine is available to the school library media specialists so that questionably blocked sites can be reviewed and immediately accessed by staff and students if found to be useful.

School library media specialists also have the ethical responsibility to help ensure patrons use the Internet in acceptable ways by:

- Helping write and enforce the district's Acceptable Use Policy
- Developing and teaching the values needed to be self-regulating Internet users
- Supervising, and possibly limiting, computers with Internet access and making sure all adults who monitor networked computers are knowledgeable about the Internet
- Educating and informing parents and the public about school Internet uses and issues
- Creating a learning environment that promotes the use of the Internet for accomplishing resource-based activities to meet curricular objectives

I have to admit that after crusading for nearly six years for filter-free Internet access for my school district and then being forced by CIPA to install a filter, the sun still rises. And in some sense, I believe our schools are more ethically responsible for using a limited filtering system that keeps the little ones from accidentally accessing inappropriate Web sites. When configured and monitored as accurately as possible, our filter becomes a selection, rather than censorship tool. But I am watching it very closely.

ALA Library Code of Ethics Statement III

ALA Library Code of Ethics Statement III: *We protect each library user's right to privacy and confidentiality with respect to information sought or received and resources consulted, borrowed, acquired or transmitted.*

Privacy issues are a hot-button topic as citizens become more aware of how easily technology can gather, hold, and analyze personal data and how citizens' online activities can be monitored. As a society, we weigh our individual need for privacy against our need for security and convenience. Schools reflect the societal concerns and the school library media specialist is often placed in a decision making position regarding privacy issues.

State and national laws are specific about the confidentiality of some forms of student information, including grades, health, and attendance records. Laws for 48 states and the District of Columbia that address the confidentiality of library records can be found on ALA's Office of Intellectual Freedom Web site <www.ala.org/alaorg/oif/stateprivacylaws.html>. The Family Educational Rights and Privacy Act (FERPA) is a federal law that addresses student educational privacy rights. School board policies address student privacy rights and these policies should comply with federal and state laws.

While the school library media specialist needs to be aware of the general laws and board policies regarding student data privacy issues, the ethical choices we must make about giving student library usage information may fall outside the parameters of legally or policy defined "education records." Circulation records, Internet use logs, and other professional observations generally do not fit the description of an "education record." State laws referring to library records may not be interpreted as applicable to school library media center records. (Please remember, I am not a lawyer, although I sometimes play one in chat rooms.)

Adding complexity to ethical choices that must be made in interpreting the general statement about a library patron's right to privacy, minors have traditionally been accorded fewer privacy rights than adults. To what extent do we, as school library media specialists, reveal the information-seeking and reading habits of an individual student to other adults who have a custodial (and ethical) responsibility for the well being of that student? Do I let a child's parent, teacher, or school counselor know if one of my students has been accessing "how to" suicide materials on the Web? Do I give information to an authority on a child's Internet use if it appears that the authority is just on a "fishing trip" with little probable cause for needing this data?

There are often legitimate pedagogical reasons to share information about a child's library resource use with that child's teachers. Is the child selecting reading materials at a level that allows that child to practice his or her reading skills? Is the child using the online resources to complete a classroom assignment?

Most of us can agree that violating the privacy of our students for our own convenience (displaying overdue lists that link student names with specific materials on the library bulletin board, school Web site, or sending such information to parents directly) is unethical. Blindly supplying information about student reading or browsing habits to any adult who requests such information would also be a violation. Finer guidelines need to be established if we are to act ethically in the broader context of student and school welfare.

I would suggest we ask ourselves as school library media specialists when making decisions about student privacy issues:

- What are my school's policies and state and federal laws regarding the confidentiality of student information? Have I consulted with and can I expect support from my administration regarding decisions I make regarding student privacy? Is there recourse to the school's legal counsel regarding difficult or contentious issues?
- What is the legitimate custodial responsibility of the person or group asking for information about a student?
- How accurately and specifically can I provide that information?
- By providing such information, is there a reasonable chance the information may prevent some harm either to the individual or to others in the school or community?
- Is there a legitimate pedagogical reason to share student information with a teacher? Am I sharing information about materials that students are using for curricular purposes or for personal use?
- Have I clearly stated to my students what the library guidelines are on the release of personal information? If the computers in the library are or can be remotely monitored, is there a clear statement of that fact readily posted?
- If student activity on a computer is logged, are students aware of this record, how long the log is kept, how the log may be used, and by whom?

As school library media specialists, we of course need to help students be aware of technology issues related to privacy so that they can protect their own privacy and honor the privacy of others. Students need to understand that businesses and organizations use information to market products and that information is often gathered electronically, both overtly and covertly. Students need to know that a stranger is a stranger, whether met on the playground or on the Internet, and that personal information shared with a stranger may put them and their families at risk. Students need to know that schools have the right to search their files when created and stored on school owned computer hardware. Students need to be taught to respect the privacy of others: because information is displayed on a computer screen doesn't make it public; and information inadvertently left accessible does not mean that it is appropriate to access it.

We need to help the school set good guidelines. Helen Adam's booklet *The Internet Invasion: Is Privacy at Risk* lists six specific school topics related to privacy (2002), and the school library media specialist should understand the privacy issues surrounding each and be able to help make good school policy related to them:

1. Addressing privacy in an Acceptable Use Policy
2. Displaying privacy policies or statements on district Web sites
3. Identifying students on district Web sites
4. Making student records available electronically
5. Conducting market research on students
6. Students providing personal information about themselves

As Adams reminds us, "This is one of the gray areas for thinking individuals to ponder" (personal e-mail, 2002).

ALA Library Code of Ethics Statement IV

ALA Library Code of Ethics Statement IV: *We recognize and respect intellectual property rights.*

It is hard to remember, but intellectual property theft existed prior to electronic cutting and pasting, peer-to-peer music sharing services, and free term paper sites. It is just that the speed, availability, and ease with which property can be copied have all led to greater instances of piracy, plagiarism, and even disdain for copyright laws.

The school library media specialist has an ethical responsibility to help students understand that property is a two-sided issue: they need to respect the property of others as well as protect their own property from the abuses of others. Students need to know about the unethical practices of others and how to protect themselves from those practices. Students need to know that copyright laws protect their original work and that they have a right to give or not give permission for others to use it. Students need to know that passwords must be kept confidential to prevent the unauthorized access to a student's data as well as to help ensure a student's privacy.

However, the major challenge for the school library media specialist is helping teachers stem the tide of plagiarism, exacerbated by new technologies, washing through our schools. One study reports that more than half of those high school students surveyed acknowledged downloading a paper from the Internet or copying text without proper attribution (eSchool News, 2002).

While we need to acknowledge this is a serious problem, teachers and librarians trying to "catch" plagiarism in student work are expending too much effort. Using various Web services such as Turnitin.com™ and using search engines to determine if or how much of student writing is lifted from online sources are primary means of addressing the plagiarism issue.

Ethically, we need to spend the greatest share of our time in preventing plagiarism before it happens. This can and should be done in a number of ways:

- By teaching:
  - What plagiarism is
  - When and why to paraphrase
  - When using another's words is appropriate
  - How to cite all formats of sources
- By having a school or district-wide "cheating" policy that includes the definition and consequences for plagiarism
- By creating "assignments worth doing"

Our time as school library media specialists and educators is best spent in creating assignments that minimize the likelihood of plagiarism. Rather than making assignments that can be easily plagiarized and then contriving methods for detecting or reducing copying, we should be spending our time with teachers planning projects that require original, thoughtful research. Some attributes of research assignments that authentically reduce the likelihood of plagiarism include:

1. They have a clarity of educational purpose readily shared with and understood by the student.
2. The students themselves have a choice of research topic or research emphasis.
3. They are related to topics relevant to students' lives and experiences or to the community in which the students live.
4. The results of the research may be shared in a narrative rather than an expository style of writing, and the results include

observations about the research process as well as the research conclusions.

5. They stress higher level thinking skills of application, analysis, synthesis, and evaluation and promote creative solutions to problems

6. The research answers real questions or helps solve genuine problems.

7. The completion of the information-seeking project requires a variety of information finding activities including primary research for a complete response.

8. Research units include "hands-on" activities such as using technology to communicate the findings or allowing a multi-sensory approach to communicating the findings.

9. Projects require cooperation or collaboration by teams of students.

10. The results of students' research are shared with an audience beyond the teacher and the classroom.

11. The projects have clearly stated assessment criteria that are given at the time of the assignment. The criteria address creativity and originality as quality indicators.

12. The units are structured and monitored in such a way that students are given the opportunity to review, revise, reflect, and improve on the product throughout the research process.

We need to acknowledge that when students plagiarize, they are not just violating the ethical principles of intellectual property, but they also are not learning the skills needed to successfully solve problems and answer questions. If those critical skills are not taught and practiced, the school library media specialist may have violated an even greater professional ethic.

ALA Library Code of Ethics Statement V

ALA Library Code of Ethics Statement V: *We treat co-workers and other colleagues with respect, fairness and good faith, and advocate conditions of employment that safeguard the rights and welfare of all employees of our institutions.*

The introduction of technology into our libraries and schools has given an interesting twist to our collegial relationships. We have one role that has grown in importance, staff trainer, and another that has grown in complexity, staff watchdog.

As among the first in schools to make productive use of technologies, our role that *Information Power* describes as "Instructional Partner" has increased in importance. For many school library media specialists, we are expected to teach not just students, but staff members, the productive uses of technology. We have a responsibility to our co-workers to teach safe and ethical technology use along with simple "how to's"—just like with our students. Protecting one's privacy, guarding one's property, and stressing the safe use of technologies, especially the Internet, are now some of the most important ways we "safeguard the rights and welfare of all employees of our institutions." Sharing our expertise in the ethical use of information and technology is how we treat other educators with "respect, fairness, and good faith."

It has always been a part of our job to help ensure legal technology use by both staff and students in our district, not just through training, but by monitoring as well. This is not a task most of us would choose for ourselves, but one that is thrust upon us because of the resources we control. Being asked by a staff member to make unauthorized copies of print and audiovisual materials, to load software on more workstations than the licenses permit, or to set up a showing of a videotape that falls outside of public performance parameters is not an uncommon experience. In these cases, most of us have learned to quietly, politely, and firmly just say "no" and explain how such an action violates not only the law but also our personal and professional ethical codes. A gentle reminder of how our own attitudes and examples as educators toward intellectual property set a powerful example for our students is also usually in order.

At some point, our knowledge of the violation of copyright or materials licensing by a colleague may become so egregious that we need to inform an administrator of the problem. We have an ethical duty to do so despite the uncomfortable position in which it places us. No district can guarantee that its staff is in perfect legal compliance with copyright, but a district and all of its employees do have the obligation to exercise due diligence in enforcing copyright laws by establishing policies, training staff, and taking disciplinary action when infractions are known. Large fines are given to districts that make no attempt or implicitly encourage copyright violation. Actions or inactions that lead to scarce school dollars spent on fines rather than student resources are unethical indeed.

Most schools' Acceptable Use Policies (AUP) also forbid the use of school resources for non-school uses. However, more often than not, it may be best to turn a blind eye to personal use unless it is blatantly inappropriate and public. We need to strictly prohibit the use or distribution of pornography or any image that co-workers might regard as creating a hostile work environment. The school library media specialist should not tolerate harassment or entrepreneurship conducted using school networks by anyone.

But we do need to recognize that teachers e-mail their kids in college, explore possible vacation destinations, or place an online order to Land's End now and again. We need to recognize that these folks are professionals, that lessons will be planned, and that homework will be graded whether at school during a prep time or at the kitchen table after supper. It is the nature of professionals. Moreover, professionals need to be accorded professional respect.

So why not take the hard line approach to enforcing a school AUP? It has everything to do with climate. Unless it affects job performance, personal Internet use makes the school a more enjoyable place to work. Teachers have enough stress in their lives. A little humor lessens the stress, makes for a happier teacher, and this is a good thing. After all, would you want your child with an *unhappy* teacher?

We cannot throw out the rules. We have a professional, legal, and ethical responsibility to enforce board adopted policies. We cannot tolerate Internet use in schools that involves harassment, encourages malingering, or supports a personal business. However, we can and should recognize that schools are comprised of human beings. Moreover, we need to do everything we can to make school a respectful, people-friendly place for both staff and students.

ALA Library Code of Ethics Statement VI

ALA Library Code of Ethics Statement VI: *We do not advance private interests at the expense of library users, colleagues, or our employing institutions.*

In a school setting, I cannot say that I've had much chance to violate this sixth standard. I've never been offered a huge sum of cash or an exotic vacation in exchange for purchasing a grossly inferior encyclopedia instead of the *World Book* or *Grolier's*. It's probably just as well.

Gerhardt in her comments on this statement asks if accepting vendor purchased meals at conferences, adding vacation days to out-of-town conferences, or working on professional organization duties during school time violates this ethical standard. These infractions seem to be small potatoes in a world of political "contributions" and school boards being wined-and-dined in luxurious settings by big technology companies. My own conscience is not troubled doing any of these things *in moderation*.

Regardless of the amount of discretionary funds at our disposal, we do have an ethical obligation to practice open service and equipment procurement practices, accurate curriculum mapping, review-driven material selection practices, and detailed budgeting. When budgets are tight, the selection of resources for their specific value to students and the educational program becomes even more critical. Convenience, charm of salespersons, or the lure of that free calendar simply should not enter into the choice of one product over another. And seeing long rows of gourmet cookbooks on the shelves of an elementary school library genuinely distresses me. And those were ordered for whom?

A combination of new and expensive technologies, modest pay in the teaching profession, and a national spirit of entrepreneurship has created an environment in which some educators, including librarians, may be tempted to use school resources for personal gain. Establishing a Web site for a personal business on the school server, using school e-mail to close a deal, or using computer equipment to do non-school or projects for pay certainly qualify as advancing "private interests at the expense of … our employing institutions." We need to carefully separate the time, equipment, and supplies we use as school employees from those we use for any private business or non-school volunteer activities we may undertake.

Our time is also a resource. Ethically we are bound to use the time we are at work in the service of our school, our staff, and our students. We need to conscientiously eliminate what Steven Covey in his book *The Seven Habits of Highly Effective People* would identify as Quadrant III or Quadrant IV activities toward Quadrant II activities: those that are not urgent, but are important such as long-term planning, relationship building, and communications. We need to differentiate between our professional duties and those technical and clerical duties.

Most of us work in tax-supported institutions and have the obligation not just to be wise and honest in our expenditure of public funds but to avoid the appearance of any wrong-doing as well.

ALA Library Code of Ethics Statement VII

ALA Library Code of Ethics Statement VII: *We distinguish between our personal convictions and professional duties and do not allow our personal beliefs to interfere with fair representation of the aims of our institutions or the provision of access to their information resources.*

Distinguishing between our personal convictions and professional duties is one of the narrower tight ropes we walk as school library media specialists. The addition of information technologies into schools and libraries has not made upholding this standard any easier. This statement should be addressed on two levels: policy and resources.

Policy

I hear many concerns and questions about information access policies, especially from teachers and librarians who believe their school guidelines are too restrictive. Should students have access to e-mail? To chat rooms? To music and video files? How much printing should a student be able to do? For what purposes? Should students be able to use the Internet to play games? To check sports scores? To find jokes and pictures of questionable taste? Technology has made circulation rules (three books per student) seem quite simple.

As was stated earlier, good rules should reflect the philosophy of the institution and create ownership of the library program by staff, students, and parents. A good advisory committee that has as one of its charges oversight of library rules can help do this. The technician or IT manager whose responsibility includes network maintenance and security is an important member of such a committee. When the lines of communication open up between those whose expertise is in technology and those whose expertise is in education, intelligent, workable rules for student and staff result. If a teacher, student, or parent disagrees with a library policy, reconsideration of the policy by the advisory committee is an effective means of addressing such a difference.

Resources

We owe it to our students and staff to keep our personal feelings on issues from restricting their access to information. *(Remember Ethical Statement I? We provide the highest level of service to all library users through ... accurate, unbiased, and courteous responses to all requests.)*

I have political biases. Ask me about gun control, abortion, immigration policies, homosexuality, mass transportation, global-warming, or the President, and I will happily give you my opinions — some more informed than others. As a librarian, I have prided myself in not allowing my personal convictions about specific topics to dictate the range of materials I make available to users.

This seemed to be relatively easy when our libraries offered users a limited range of print resources. If I ordered the SIRS Research folders, Facts-On-File titles, and Opposing Viewpoints books along with both *The Nation* and *The National Review* magazines, I thought I had all sides of most controversial issues covered.

The Internet and online services have given us access to an unimaginable spectrum of opinions, now readily available to students and staff in even the smallest of school library media centers. Scholars, pundits, wackos, and seventh graders all can and do publish "information" online, undistinguishable by appearance or availability. The information presented by businesses, nonprofits, "think-tanks," and other sites may be accurate but heavily biased.

I am rapidly concluding that there is no "supported" belief that cannot be found on the Internet. (Want a recipe for spotted owls? It's easily found.)

While the availability of misinformation or biased opinions is often confusing or can lead researchers to make choices or form opinions that are embarrassing, there is a profound and very serious dimension to this issue as well. Increasingly students are using the Internet to meet personal needs and for school assignments that ask them to solve genuine problems. Making good consumer choices, health decisions, and career choices are parts of many districts' curricula. Gaining historical background and perspectives on social, scientific, and political issues through research is a common task expected by many teachers.

Ethically, we cannot rely on the "free" Internet alone to meet the information needs of our patrons. The availability of resources that have been edited and selected for their authority is perhaps more essential than ever. It is our ethical duty to provide print reference and trade materials at reading levels accessible to the age of the student, a range of periodicals related to the curriculum and personal interests, and subscriptions to online resources, such as content specific databases and full-text periodical databases. We also must teach students about and facilitate their access to materials that are available through interlibrary loan.

Even more importantly, we need to teach our library users to be able to evaluate information for themselves. Were I the Grand Panjandrum of Libraries, I would instantly add Johnson's IXth Statement to ALA's Code of Ethics: *We teach our library users to be critical users of information.*

Some established guidelines for the accuracy and reliability of information seem relatively simple to teach:

- **Authority.** Who compiled this information or offered this opinion and what is author's expertise?
- **Age.** How old is the information?
- **Verifiability.** Is the information or the opinion found similar to that in other information sources?
- **Bias.** What is the reason the information has been compiled or the opinion has been offered? Does the author have some vested interest in the reader sharing his or her opinion? Who sponsors this site and how might the sponsor profit from convincing a reader to form specific beliefs?

Establishing the "authority" of information sources dealing with controversial social issues can be challenging if the school library media specialist wishes to honor the religious or political views of a student's family, especially when those views differ radically from one's own. Commentaries on environmental issues, for example, offered on National Public Radio's *Talk of the Nation* and on the *Rush Limbaugh Show* may be seen by some parents, by some teachers, and by oneself as having differing degrees of value and reliability. This is compounded by the degree to which people at both ends of the political spectrum are more reliant on dogma or doctrine than on a thoughtful review of evidence to help them make decisions.

Yet as ethical educators, we need to ask students to support their conclusions and be able to defend the sources of the information with which they have chosen to do so. If parents are sufficiently uncomfortable with the spirit of open inquiry as a part of education, I believe they should consider enrolling their children in a non-public school that reflects their specific sets of beliefs.

For countries like ours, founded on democratic freedoms and individual choices, the ability to analyze information should be the most important goal of our schools.

ALA Library Code of Ethics Statement VIII

ALA Library Code of Ethics Statement VIII: *We strive for excellence in the profession by maintaining and enhancing our own knowledge and skills, by encouraging the professional development of co-workers, and by fostering the aspirations of potential members of the profession.*

While we do need to practice and help others practice the standards of ethical behaviors I–VII, statement VIII, for those of us in education, supercedes them all. Our primary ethical responsibility is promoting meaningful change in our institutions.

Technology is used as a catalyst for change in education in the best and worst senses of the word. It has opened avenues toward previously undreamt of information and communication opportunities. It is spurring some teachers to be more creative, more constructivist-based, and more individualized in their instruction. The chance of technology being used badly is also great as critics like The Alliance for Childhood, Jane Healy, Larry Cuban, and Clifford Stoll suggest. Technology can depersonalize education, can divert funds from more effective educational practices, and can over-emphasize low-level skill attainment as the ultimate educational goal.

As school library media specialists, we understand perhaps better than many in education that teaching is a moral pursuit. It is changing the world in a positive way through changing lives of our students in positive way. We must recognize technology simply as a tool that will help us achieve those changes.

Too many of our schools lack effective leadership for the positive changes that technology can foster or accelerate. In such situations, a clear vision of what technology can and should be doing, well articulated by the school library media specialist, can have a tremendous impact. We can and should help fill such a directional void. The school library media specialist makes an especially effective change agent because:

- Our programs affect the whole school climate
- We advocate information skills and personalized learning for every child
- We advocate for technology being used to promote problem solving and higher level thinking
- We have no subject area biases or territories to protect
- We are extremely charming

While often uncomfortable, the school library media specialist must challenge the system to be an effective agent for change. We do so by working on school governing committees, leading staff development activities, and exemplifying great teaching practices and technology use ourselves. We are involved in curriculum revision and fight for the effective integration of technology and information literacy skills. We write for district newsletters and talk to parent and community organizations. We hold offices in unions and other professional organizations. We write to legislators and attend political functions and school board meetings. We form strong networks with like-minded reformers inside and outside our profession. Throughout these efforts, we keep firmly in mind that technology's purpose is to empower our students.

Our role as the "teacher of teachers" has never been greater, as was alluded to in Statement V. We need to lead formal staff development activities, to work on long-term staff development plans, and to serve as mentors and peer-coaches in our schools. The school library media specialist is especially effective in working with teachers on the meaningful integration of technology into the curriculum through instructional units that include information literacy skills and stress higher-level thinking and by designing authentic assessments of performance-based units of instruction. We are the team players, the hand-holders, the encouragers, the cheerleaders, the resource-providers, and the shoulders on which to cry. We help improve our institutions by helping to improve the performance of the people who work within them.

As the tools of our profession change with technology and our mission grows to encompass teacher training and leadership, our ethical duty to upgrade our own professional skills takes on ever increasing importance. My formal education ended with a master's degree in 1979 from an excellent ALA accredited program. This was before personal computers of any usefulness; before popular use of OPACs; before online databases; before the acceptance of the Internet by the bourgeoisie; before multimedia encyclopedias; before the printing press (well, not quite).

It follows that our ethical duty also includes membership and participation in professional associations that are devoted to ongoing professional development and attendance at the conferences and workshops they offer. We must continue to read professional journals and books. We must take advantage of listservs and other forms of electronic communication that help us maintain virtual conversations about our practice.

As Statement VIII concludes, we must foster "the aspirations of potential members of the profession." A person recently commented to me that one must be mad to go into school librarianship. He is right, of course, on a number of levels. You have to mad (passionate) for stories, computers, and especially working with kids. You have to be mad (angry) about how poorly our schools underserve too many vulnerable children. Finally, you have to be mad (crazy) enough to believe that you as one individual have the power to change your institution, your political systems, and especially, the lives of your students and teachers. It is a rightful part of our ethical code that we must recruit other madmen and madwomen to our profession.

We should all be on, as the Blues Brothers describe it, "a mission from God" *every day* to make sure technology use in our schools is actually improving the lives of our students and staff. Heaven knows that nobody goes into the profession to make money. As educators, our satisfaction comes from actually believing we are doing something that will make the world a more humane place in which to live. The ultimate ethic of our practice is improving the lives of the children who attend our schools. The addition of technology to our schools does not change this; in fact, it may just make it more imperative. Minnesota writer, Frederick Manfred in his poem "What About You, Boy?" says it far better than I ever could:

> … Open up and let go.
> Even if it's only blowing. But blast.
> And I say this loving my God.
> Because we are all he has at last.
> So what about it, boy?
> Is your work going well?
> Are you still lighting lamps
> Against darkness and hell?

Conclusion

It is a dangerous thing to set oneself up as an "expert" about ethics. Others hold one to very high ethical standards and there always seem to be folks sniffing about for hypocritical behavior on the "expert's" part. One runs the chance of appearing holier-than-thou and of having folks feel uncomfortable in one's presence. Probably the worst thing is that one quickly realizes there are few ethical absolutes, and one is regarded as an anal-retentive or as a godless situational relativist depending on the audience. Ethics is an interesting and important topic, which needs to be brought out into the sunshine and aired on a regular basis if we are to do our jobs well.

In the end, the best thing we can do is to be thoughtful and to listen to our consciences. As human beings, we constantly make moral judgments, decide issues of right and wrong, and attempt to determine what behaviors are humane and inhumane. We want to feel both our professional and personal actions and attitudes:

- Promote the general health of society
- Maintain or increase individual rights and freedoms
- Protect individuals from harm
- Treat all human beings as having an inherent value and accord those beings respect
- Uphold religious, social, cultural, and government laws and mores

In other words, we want the decisions we make to not only not have a damaging impact on ourselves, on those we serve, or on our society but to improve our world as well.

I am proud to be a member of a profession that takes its ethical responsibilities seriously.

Works Cited

Adams, H. (2002). *The Internet Invasion: Is Privacy at Risk?* Rev. ed. Follett's Professional Development Series.

eSchool News Staff. (2002). *Kentucky school finds seniors lifted text from the Internet.* eSchool News. July 1. Retrieved September 5, 2002 from <http://www.eschoolnews.com/news/showStory.cfm?ArticleID=3824>.

Gerhardt, L. (1990). "Ethical back talk: Chewing on ALA's Code." *School Library Journal.* 36(2), 4.

Gerhardt, L. (1990). "Ethical back talk: I." *School Library Journal.* 36(2), 4.

Gerhardt, L. (1990). "Ethical back talk: II." *School Library Journal.* 36(4), 4.

Gerhardt, L. (1990). "Ethical back talk: III." *School Library Journal.* 36(6), 4.

Gerhardt, L. (1990). "Ethical back talk: IV." *School Library Journal.* 36(8), 4.

Gerhardt, L. (1990). "Ethical back talk: V." *School Library Journal.* 36(10), 4.

Gerhardt, L. (1990). "Ethical back talk: VI." *School Library Journal.* 36(12), 4.

Gerhardt, L. (1991). "Ethical back talk: VI." *School Library Journal.* 37(1), 4.

Discussion Questions

1. Ethically, how should the librarian respond to challenges to the AUP? Does strict enforcement of the AUP always meet the ethics of the profession? Why or why not?

2. Part of the information literacy curriculum of your district requires that students evaluate Web sites to determine the validity, accuracy, and currency of information located. To accomplish this goal, students evaluate several Web sites related to controversial issues. They are asked to identify propaganda, hyperbole, and red herrings. A parent group objects to the use of these Web sites saying that the school is promoting the points of view of the organizations whose Web sites are used in the exercise. How can you ethically defend the use of Web sites that promote socially unacceptable points of view?

3. Since Internet filtering is required by the Children's Internet Protection Act (CIPA) if a school receives any federal funding, describe a process by which you can comply with the act yet still meet the ethical obligation of access to information in all formats. Is this ideal process compatible with the thinking in your school district?

4. What is the ethical implication of access to technology when faced with significantly inadequate budget for library materials? How would one justify not purchasing needed print materials in favor of technology resources?

5. Technology enables students and teachers to compromise the intellectual property of many individuals and corporations. The school librarian is often asked to assist in reproduction, manipulation, and distribution of this intellectual property, often with admirable goals such as rewarding highly successful students or promoting academic achievement. What should be the ethical response of the librarian when asked to lead or participate in these activities? How can such a stance be defended in the light of the stated goals?

Chapter Six
Ethics and Intellectual Freedom
By Carrie Gardner

*H*arry Potter and the Sorcerer's Stone by J.K. Rowling, *The Bible, The Giver* by Lois Lowry, and the *Merriam-Webster Collegiate Dictionary* share a number of common themes. They can all be found in thousands of school libraries across this country and they have all had their suitability for inclusion in a school library challenged. In some cases, they have been removed from school library collections and from the access of young people (Doyle, 2001, 22, 66, 85).

Definition

The ALA Office for Intellectual Freedom provides the following formal definition: "Intellectual Freedom is the right of every individual to both seek and receive information from all points of view without restriction. It provides free access to all expressions of ideas through which all sides of a question, cause, or movement may be explored. Intellectual Freedom encompasses the freedom to hold, receive and disseminate ideas" (ALA, 2002).

In order for intellectual freedom to exist, a number of factors integral to school libraries must both support and nurture intellectual freedom in the form of access.

■ **Collection**
   In order for the patrons of a school library media center to experience intellectual freedom, the collection of print and non-print resources — including those available via electronic networks — must span the range of human knowledge and expression.

■ **People**
   All adult and student workers in a school library media center respect the rights of all patrons (student and adult) to access, to print, and to check out the information desired. This is done without questioning the motives of the patron.

■ **Climate**

The most important, yet fragile, factor is that of climate. In order for patrons of a school library media center to enjoy intellectual freedom, they must feel as if the climate of the library supports and defends their right to access the information they need to complete their studies or the information they want to fulfill an information need. Benchmarks by which a negative intellectual freedom climate can be measured include posted signs designed to limit students' behavior as they seek information, accusatory tones used to inquire about "why" someone needs information, restrictions on the use of materials, and restrictions on checking out materials.

The Users of a School Library Media Center

Both adults and students use school library media centers. For the purpose of this chapter, the focus will be on student patrons. Adult patrons of school library media centers are much more likely to have the transportation and the financial resources they need to solve their information needs with or without the resources of a school library media center. School students do not necessarily have access to the transportation and the financial resources needed to fulfill their information needs in other libraries or via the purchase of resources.

Students from grades kindergarten to approximately tenth grade are not legally able to drive and therefore face a huge barrier to using a library other than their school library media center. At this point in American society, most students do not live within walking distance of a public library, and those few who do are restricted from walking there because of safety concerns. Parents rarely feel comfortable allowing their elementary or middle school students to walk more than a few blocks from their homes.

Financial resources of students in grades K–10 are also limited. When faced with an urgent information need, adults will often rely on their financial resources in order to purchase the information they need. Examples of this can be found in everyday life. Adults buy books so they can do their own income taxes, can learn about illnesses, and can pursue their hobbies. Bookstores, and specifically sections such as self-help and medical information, exist because of adults' desires to have information at hand when they wish to access it. Students, the main patron group of school library media centers, usually do not have the financial resources to purchase the information they need in order to complete their studies or to fulfill the information needs that arise in their lives. The influence of finances and transportation dictate that in order for a school library media program to be successful, school library media specialists must constantly work to discover the information needs of the students and must work to provide access to that information via the school library.

Characteristics of Our Students

American school students are the perfect mirrors of a very imperfect society. When discussing intellectual freedom and students, it is necessary to discuss the issues facing them. Our children are not growing up with Mr. and Mrs. Brady solving major problems in 30 minutes or Ward and June Cleaver being the perfect parents in perfect preppy clothing. Instead, our students are growing up in families that face mental illness, alcoholism, drug addition, poverty, busy working parents, and a world with 24 hour news sources bringing the worlds' problems to our television sets and computers. The Children's Defense Fund provides the following facts on today's youth (Children's, 2002):

- One in two will live in a single parent family at some point in childhood.
- One in three is born to unmarried parents.
- One in three will be poor at some point in their childhood.
- One in three is behind a year or more in school.
- One in four lives with only one parent.
- Two in five never complete a single year of college.
- One in five was born poor.
- One in five is born to a mother who did not graduate from high school.
- One in five has a foreign-born mother.
- Three in five preschoolers have their mother in the labor force.
- One in six is poor now.
- One in six is born to a mother who did not receive prenatal care in the first three months of pregnancy.
- One in seven has no health insurance.
- One in seven has a worker in their family but still is poor.
- One in eight lives in a family receiving food stamps.
- One in eight never graduates from high school.
- One in eight is born to a teenage mother.
- One in 12 has a disability.
- One in 13 was born with low birth weight.
- One in 15 lives at less than half the poverty level.
- One in 24 lives with neither parent.

- One in 26 is born to a mother who received late or no prenatal care.
- One in 60 sees his or her parents divorce in any year.
- One in 139 will die before his or her first birthday.
- One in 1,056 will be killed by guns before age 20.

The Children's Defense Fund also tells us that *every day* in America:

- One young person under 25 dies from HIV infection
- Five children or youth under 20 commit suicide
- Nine children or youth under 20 are homicide victims
- Nine children or youth under 20 die from firearms
- 34 children and youth under 20 die from accidents
- 77 babies die
- 157 babies are born at very low birth weight (less than three lbs., four oz.)
- 180 children are arrested for violent crimes
- 367 children are arrested for drug abuse
- 401 babies are born to mothers who had late or no prenatal care
- 825 babies are born at low birth weight (less than five lbs., eight oz.)
- 1,310 babies are born without health insurance
- 1,329 babies are born to teen mothers
- 2,019 babies are born into poverty
- 2,319 babies are born to mothers who are not high school graduates
- 2,861 high school students drop out
- 3,585 babies are born to unmarried mothers
- 4,248 children are arrested
- 7,883 children are reported abused or neglected
- 17,297 public school students are suspended

These statistics provide school library media specialists with valuable information. We know that students in our schools are living the lives to which these statistics refer and, therefore, have information needs about these topics. Providing student access to fiction books that explore these issues and to nonfiction books that provide information and access to Internet-based resources are critical functions of a school library media specialist. This is true for two major reasons.

First, Maslow's Hierarchy of Needs tells us that if our students cannot effectively process the issues and events in their lives, they will not be receptive to the education the school system (of which the school library is a part) is trying to provide for the child (1999). Having information about a problem empowers the person with that problem to feel as if the situation is not hopeless and there are solutions. Once a student feels that there are plausible solutions to the issues facing him or her and loved ones, the student is able to focus on the educational activities involved with formal schooling.

Second, our students study the major issues facing us as a society and a world. Our youngest students now need information about drugs, addiction, sexual abuse, abortion, capital punishment, terrorism, religions, and so on in order to complete their school assignments. Educators have learned that if they use the major social issues in order to gain and maintain the attention of our students, students learn more. We as a society have also made the decision that topics such as drug education will be taught as part of our formal K–12 schooling process. Because of these factors, student assignments require the school library media center to collect and disseminate information about controversial topics that often make adults uncomfortable.

Selection, Censorship, and Intellectual Freedom

Society has given librarians the task of collecting, maintaining, preserving, and providing access to information. Librarians have the power to hide information by cataloging it in obscure places with non-descriptive subject headings, by keeping it on restrictive shelves, by requiring permission slips for access, or by not acquiring it at all. School librarians are no exception. We have the power to prevent ideas from reaching our student patrons with our selection policies and procedures.

In the middle of the 20th century, Lester Asheim, a great mind in Library Science, wrote a groundbreaking essay on this subject: *Not Censorship but Selection*. He articulated the unique role librarians play in the dissemination of knowledge. His points include:

- Librarians should look for reasons to include information, not exclude it.
- Fiscal resources should not be employed as an excuse not to purchase resources.
- Librarians must recognize their own biases and compensate for them during the collection process.
- Perceived or real threats of censorship attacks or other action should not influence the selection process (Asheim, [n.d.]).

This essay provides philosophical underpinnings for library programs. The American Library Association has created and maintained a series of documents designed to explain how librarians provide the highest level of service to patrons. The Intellectual Freedom Committee of the American Library Association maintains the documents, the Library Bill of Rights.

The Library Bill of Rights and Its Interpretations

During the 1930s, Forrest Spaulding, a librarian at the Des Moines Public Library was concerned that patrons were not receiving appropriate services and resources. He wrote the first draft of the Library Bill of Rights (LBR). The Des Moines, Iowa, Public Library Board adopted the document on November 21, 1938. The American Library Association council at the Annual Conference adopted the document in 1939 (ALA, 2002, 59). It has been revamped during the last few decades. The purpose of the document is to provide librarians with a set of principles by which they serve their patrons. In many ways, it is comparable to the Hippocratic Oath given to medical doctors. Librarians who follow the principles discussed in the LBR provide the highest level of service to their patrons. The Library Bill of Rights also explains a library's principles to all stakeholders, patrons, board members, and so forth.

Today, the Library Bill of Rights states:

> The American Library Association affirms that all libraries are forums for information and ideas, and that the following basic policies should guide their services.
>
> I. Books and other library resources should be provided for the interest, information, and enlightenment of all people of the community the library serves. Materials should not be excluded because of the origin, background, or views of those contributing to their creation.
>
> II. Libraries should provide materials and information presenting all points of view on current and historical issues. Materials should not be proscribed or removed because of partisan or doctrinal disapproval.
>
> III. Libraries should challenge censorship in the fulfillment of their responsibility to provide information and enlightenment.
>
> IV. Libraries should cooperate with all persons and groups concerned with resisting abridgment of free expression and free access to ideas.
>
> V. A person's right to use a library should not be denied or abridged because of origin, age, background, or views.
>
> VI. Libraries which make exhibit spaces and meeting rooms available to the public they serve should make such facilities available on an equitable basis, regardless of the beliefs or affiliations of individuals or groups requesting their use (ALA, 2002, 57).

The ALA Intellectual Freedom Committee is the ALA entity responsible for the maintenance of the Library Bill of Rights. Shortly after its adoption in the late 1930s, the Intellectual Freedom Committee began writing interpretations of the Library Bill of Rights in order to address specific actions and policies librarians were following that resulted in reduced access and, therefore, reduced intellectual freedom for patrons.

The interpretations and a brief explanation of the role they play in guiding school library media specialists in order to maintain intellectual freedom follow.

Access for Children and Young People to Videotapes and Other Nonprint Formats

Access for children and young people is often used as a reason to censor or prohibit access. Like waving flags at a Fourth of July parade, librarians and other interested parties often wave the protection of children and young people as a reason to censor. This interpretation cautions librarians to allow patrons of all ages access to information in all nonprint formats. Some librarians feel that non-book materials should not circulate beyond the physical walls of the library. Reasons include the materials are "more" fragile than a printed book, students could be irresponsible and could cause the destruction of the resource, the cost of the nonprint resource is often more than a book, and libraries should promote reading and not more video or TV viewing. Classroom teachers sometimes feel that students should not view materials before they are presented in class. School administrators may feel that parents will not want to be responsible for replacement fees connected to nonprint resources. In reality, today's students often need the information contained in nonprint resources. An example of this is information published by the United States Government. Since the mid 1990s, the government has stopped publishing many publications both in print and on CD-ROM or another nonprint format. They have moved to CD-ROM or one of the other nonprint formats. Recent information on brain research and learning styles indicates that our students may learn most effectively when they receive information visually. Receiving information via a computer screen or a video is often the most effective conduit for these students.

Access to Electronic Information, Services, and Networks

Libraries embraced delivery of information via electronic means in the early 1990s. This interpretation was written in order to explain that the highest level of access to electronic information is appropriate for all patrons. Wording covering children and youth is included in the interpretation.

Access to Library Resources and Services Regardless of Gender or Sexual Orientation

Society continues to wrestle with issues of gender and sexual orientation. This interpretation reminds librarians that regardless of the gender or orientation of an author, a work deserves to be considered for inclusion in library collections. Patrons should not be discriminated against because of gender or perceived or known sexual orientation.

School library media specialists often receive requests from students about topics related all aspects of human sexuality, including homosexuality. Because of this, it is appropriate for our collections and policies to be able to answer them. Resources are available that depict two same-sex people living as a family and raising children. Picture books, such as *Heather Has Two Mommies* (Leslea Newman, New York: Alyson Wonderland, 1989) and *Daddy's Roommate* (Michael Willhoite, New York: Alyson Wonderland, 1989), provide elementary children with stories that depict the everyday life for young people who live with two same-sex parents. These resources provide a great deal of comfort for those children from such homes. Authors such as Francesa Lia Block and Nancy Garden have written a number of fiction books appropriate for late elementary to high school students whose characters are homosexual or are exploring the issues around being homosexual.

Access to Resources and Services in the School Library Media Program

This is the most germane interpretation for school library media specialists. It provides guidance on maintaining intellectual freedom within a school setting. The committee felt the need to include a section that lists major barriers by which school students are denied access to information. They "include but are not limited to: imposing age or grade level restrictions on the use of resources, limiting the use of interlibrary loan and access to electronic information, charging fees for information in specific formats, requiring permission from parents or teachers, establishing restricted shelves or closed collections, and labeling" (ALA, 2002, 106). Some school library media specialists require permission forms from parents before they will allow students to access certain information or resources. The elementary school library in my hometown contains grades K–5. It requires a signed permission slip before a student may look at or check out any of the *Harry Potter* books by J.K. Rowling. When questioned about this, the librarian said that she read that some parents feel that the books promote witchcraft and in order to avoid having parents or community members upset with her, she decided to institute the permission slip policy. During the discussion, she admitted that she hadn't thought about the fact that some students would be denied access to the books because they wouldn't remember to have the slip signed or would lose the form.

Challenged Materials

Would-be censors often challenge materials. They may request that the material be removed from the school library media center or be placed in a restricted area that requires an adult's permission before the information is accessed. Sometimes the challenger requests that the resource be moved from one level of school to another. An example of this would be from the elementary to the middle school library media center or from the middle school to the high school library media center. Once a challenge to a resource has been made, the school district's reconsideration policy must be followed. This is usually referred to as the review process. During this time, the resource is under review.

If the resource is pulled for the review process, patrons are denied access to the resource during the time the material is under scrutiny. Because removal sometimes happens, this interpretation was written to provide guidance in ethical behavior on the part of the librarian. It cautions librarians to create and implement policies that allow resources to remain available during any reconsideration processes. Because the majority of challenges in America happen to resources in school library media centers, this interpretation is critical for school librarianship. In order to maintain access and intellectual freedom, reconsideration policies must promote access to challenged material during the time of review and must provide forums where the value of the resource to the school community is heard.

Diversity in Collection Development

Martin Luther King was jailed for his actions and ideas. Jesus Christ was killed because of his actions and beliefs. In 1900, having information about birth control methods was illegal and led to jail sentences. A woman who showed her ankles in Afghanistan in August of 2001 was guilty of a crime. Diverse ideas are part of the human experience. A key role for school library media centers is to provide access to ideas from across the spectrum. The fact that a school library media center must support curriculum initiatives often dictates that diverse opinions are represented. Examples of this include ideas expressed in literature and comparative religion courses, topics used by debate teams, and ideas explored in health classes. The last paragraph of this interpretation states: "Intellectual freedom the essence of equitable library services, provides for free access to all expressions of ideas through which any and all sides of a question, cause or movement may be explored. Toleration is meaningless without tolerance for what some may consider detestable" (ALA, 2002, 119).

Economic Barriers to Information Access

Millions of school children who patronize school library media centers live their lives in poverty. If school library media centers charge money for any service, a barrier between students and information exists. This is also true of fines for overdue resources. For some students, the threat of having to pay money is a very strong deterrent—one that prevents them from using the library media center. School librarians must strive to eliminate all fees and fines from their programs.

Evaluating Library Collections

School library media center collections must be evaluated in order for them to retain their relevance. This interpretation cautions librarians to evaluate collections in light of appropriate policies and the mission statement of the library. This interpretation cautions librarians not to use evaluation and weeding as a way to remove controversial materials. School library media specialists must evaluate resources in light of their relevance to the mission statement of the library and the school district and the accuracy of the information. It would be malpractice for a school librarian to retain resources published in 1950 that discuss the American space program or recent developments in chemistry.

Exhibit Spaces and Bulletin Boards

Because libraries often have exhibit spaces and bulletin board displays, this interpretation cautions librarians to allow and produce displays on a wide range of topics and resources. Prohibiting or restricting exhibits of controversial topics curbs the flow of ideas and information.

Expurgation of Library Materials

The Library Bill of Rights defines expurgation as "any deletion, excision, alteration, editing, or obliteration of any part of a library resource." Posts on online discussions such as LM_NET often discuss expurgation. Countless copies of Maurice Sendak's *In the Night Kitchen* have been expurgated because librarians concerned about the nude little boy have added a diaper with a pencil. Blue ballpoint pens have been used to add blue jeans to scantily clad natives in *National Geographic*. Black markers have been used to cover controversial words in works such as *Catcher in the Rye* and illustrations in art reference books. Legally, these actions are almost always a violation of copyright laws. Ethically, expurgation results in patrons having less access to information and it sends a message that certain pieces of information are off limits.

Privacy

This document is the newest interpretation. It was created in order to inform librarians about the importance of privacy in maintaining intellectual freedom. If patrons feel or know that their library usage habits may be disseminated to anyone, a major psychological barrier between patrons and information exists. School library media specialists, during the course of providing a library program to students, have access to information about the viewing and reading habits of students. That information must remain confidential, or all patrons, especially students, will severely curb the amount and content of the information they access.

Free Access to Libraries for Minors

This interpretation states: "every [any] restriction on access to, and use of, library resources, based solely on the chronological age, educational level, or legal emancipation of users violates Article V" of the Library Bill of Rights. This interpretation cautions librarians to provide information to patrons of all ages and educational levels. School library media specialists must follow this precept if patrons of school library media centers are to enjoy even the lowest levels of intellectual freedom. Patrons often want to check out resources written above their reading levels. Perhaps an adult will read it to them or maybe the young patron has a burning desire to explore the ideas in the book. Whatever the motive a young person has for wanting to access information, age should not be used as reason to prevent them from that information. Many school systems are now using computerized reading incentive programs. An example of this is the *Accelerated Reader*™ program. Students are told what reading level they are on and are asked to select resources from that reading level. The hope is that the students will master each level and will then progress to the next level at the appropriate time. School library media specialists are often called upon to make sure that students check out and read books at their levels. It is imperative that students be made aware that they must complete their computerized reading assignments that include selecting the appropriate books, but students must be allowed to check out other resources if they desire.

Intellectual Freedom Principles for Academic Libraries

College and university librarians created this interpretation for their colleagues. Interestingly, it does an excellent job of summarizing the role a library plays in a learning community and the librarian's responsibility to promote intellectual freedom. Libraries in an academic setting provide much needed information resources for both the students and the teachers. These ideals mirror those school library media specialists strive to implement for our academic communities.

Library-Initiated Programs as a Resource

Library patrons, including school library media center patrons, often have the opportunity to receive information via programs offered through the library. Patrons should not be restricted from programs. If restrictions are in place, intellectual freedom does not exist. School library media specialists must carefully examine any programs and must make sure that all students have access to them. For example, if students from learning support classes are not invited to participate in programs, they do not enjoy full access to the school library media center.

Meeting Rooms

Libraries that offer meeting room space for use by others should make that space available to everyone on an equitable basis. Usage should not be denied because of the content or beliefs of those wishing to use a meeting room. School library media centers rarely offer meeting room space to anyone outside of the immediate school community, but the principles put forth in this interpretation provide valuable guidelines that, when followed, guarantee that meeting rooms are equitably available. If school library meeting rooms are made available to the local Youth for Christ meetings, then they should also be accessible to groups who practice other religions, including, for example, Islam.

Restricted Access to Library Materials

Many school library media specialists have "restricted shelves." Items are placed on these shelves for a number of reasons. Some of these reasons include controversial subject matter, graphic illustrations, a history of being challenged, and even discipline problems caused by the resource. Scores of different "rules" govern these restricted collections. Some school library media specialists require a parental signature in order for a student patron to see a resource from a restricted collection; others require students to reach a certain chronological age or grade level. Still others require a teacher or an administrator to vouch for the student. The very act of placing resources on a restricted shelf infringes on the intellectual freedom of patrons. A set of barriers, usually physical and policy based, stands between the information and the patron. This interpretation cautions against engaging in restricting access to information. If the school reconsideration policy has been followed and the result is the removal or restriction of a resource, the school library media specialist is legally bound to follow that directive.

School library media specialists may find themselves in charge of a library with a wide age range and, therefore, a wide range of resources. School libraries may cover K–8, 6–12, or another combination of age ranges that requires a wide range of resources. Because of this factor, school librarians may find themselves in the position of having a patron wish to check out or access a resource meant for students who are much older or much younger than the patron. For example, a school library media specialist who has a K–5 or K–8 library may have a primary student who wants to check out a large chapter book or a book that is usually checked out by older students. Keeping in mind the principles of intellectual freedom, that some students have family members who read "thick" books to them and that some students are "ready to receive" information before an adult thinks they are, school librarians must develop a philosophy on how to handle these situations. School librarians will often ask the youngster if he or she wants "such a thick book" or if someone will help to read it. Explaining to a youngster that there is information in the book meant for older students sometimes provides the youngster with needed reader guidance. In the end, the choice about what to check out should rest with the student.

Statement on Labeling

This interpretation defines labeling as the practice of describing or designating materials by affixing a prejudicial label or by segregating them by a prejudicial system (ALA, 2002, 184). Librarians often label resources in an effort to help patrons select resources. For example, we segregate fiction and nonfiction. The motive for this action is to assist the patron, not prohibit access. We often create an "easy book" fiction section, which is also designed to help our youngest patrons retrieve information that is both on their interest and reading levels. By creating an "easy book" fiction section, some older students may feel "stupid" if they desire or need a book from the "easy book" section. The use of labels can inadvertently provide a psychological barrier to information.

Any use of labels to discriminate against patrons' access to information is a direct assault on the intellectual freedom of patrons. This happens when labels are used to prevent certain users from accessing information because of an assigned label. All library patrons should be allowed to check out books from all sections and with any labels. If librarians restrict certain patrons to the "easy book" section, they are restricting the access of patrons. If high school students are prevented from checking out a picture book, their intellectual freedom is compromised.

Society has adopted this type of system in many areas. For example, major movie theater chains enforce policies preventing viewers from watching movies with certain Motion Picture Association of America (MPAA) ratings unless they are of a certain age. Many retail establishments will not sell music or game cartridges labeled with certain ratings to a user unless the user has reached a certain chronological age. Libraries who enter into similar situations are infringing on the intellectual freedom of patrons.

A typical situation in a school library would be putting computerized reading incentive program reading levels on books and not allowing a student to check out a book unless the student were within a certain range of the target reading level. Such a practice infringes on the rights of the student to access information of his or her own choice and potentially dampers student reading by broadcasting the student's reading level to the world based on the labels on the books he or she is permitted to check out.

The Universal Right to Free Expression

The United Nations adopted the Universal Declaration of Human Rights. Article 19 of the Universal Declaration of Human Rights states: "Everyone has the right to freedom of opinion and expression, this right includes freedom to hold opinions without interference and to seek, receive and impart information and ideas through any media regardless of frontiers" (ALA, 2002, 194). This statement provides all librarians, including school library media specialists, with a fabulous summary of what intellectual freedom brings to our global society.

Legalese

The First Amendment of the United States Constitution states:

> Congress shall make no law respecting an establishment of religion or prohibiting the free exercise thereof, or abridging the freedom of speech, or of the press, or the right of the people to peaceably assemble, and to petition the government for a redress of grievances.

Thomas Jefferson, James Madison, and the other founding fathers wrote this and the other Amendments in the Bill of Rights in order to guarantee that citizens of the new country, the United States, would have rights that citizens of the British colonies did not have. Included in the First Amendment is the phrase "Congress shall make no law... abridging the freedom of speech ..." Jefferson and Madison's writings and, most importantly, court rulings determined that to have freedom of speech guaranteed in the First Amendment, American citizens are legally entitled to receive information. This legal tenet most directly affects libraries. We are in the business of supplying information to citizens, and students are most certainly citizens.

Numerous court cases have affirmed that students in American K–12 school systems have a legal right to receive information. In *Tinker v. Des Moines School District*, the Supreme Court held that school students "do not shed their constitutional rights at the schoolhouse gate" (Tinker, 1969).

Students who had worn black armbands to school in an effort to protest the Vietnam War brought this case. In *Todd v. Rochester Community Schools*, the Court of Appeals of Michigan ruled that *Slaughterhouse Five* by Kurt Vonnegut could not be banned from Michigan schools (Todd, 1972). In *Island Trees v. Pico*, the United States Supreme Court ruled that school boards do not have authority to restrict and remove books because they do not like the ideas in the books (Board, 1982). In *Case v. Unified School District*, a district removed *Annie on My Mind* by Nancy Garden. Students sued, and in 1995, the Federal District Court in Kansas found that the district had violated the students' rights under the First Amendment (Case, 1995).

Legal and Illegal Information

In America, information is legal unless it is declared illegal by an appropriate court of law. Information that has been declared illegal by American courts usually falls into one of the following categories:

- Slander: Speech that is untrue.
- Libel: Written words that are not true.
- Dangerous Speech: Speech that presents a clear and present danger to those hearing the speech in question. The most common example of dangerous speech, and that which is cited by the Supreme Court of the United States, is yelling "fire" in a crowded theatre when no such fire exists.
- Child Pornography: Information found to depict sexual conduct specified in the applicable statutes that uses images of children below specified ages.
- Obscene information: Nudity is not necessarily illegal. That is why it is possible to buy magazines such as *Playboy* and *Playgirl*. In the early part of the 20th century, American courts often declared books obscene. Examples include *Lady Chatterley's Lover* by D.H. Lawrence, *Sister Carrie* by Theodore Dreiser, and *Tropic of Cancer* by Henry Miller. By the 1960s, courts were reluctant to declare text only books obscene. By the mid 1970s, the U.S. Supreme Court had created a three prong test courts use to decide if information is obscene. In order to be declared obscene, a work must meet the following tests:
  - The average person, applying contemporary community standards, must find that the work, taken as a whole, appeals to prurient interests.

- The work must depict or describe, in a patently offensive way, sexual conduct as specified in the applicable statutes.
- The work, taken as a whole, must lack serious literary, artistic, political, or scientific value.

No one but an appropriate court of law can apply this test and can declare a work obscene. Pornography is a colloquial word that has no legal meaning, and it is used to describe sexually explicit materials.

Before the Internet, school library media specialists rarely had to worry about information that contained graphic sexual information. We debated *Forever* by Judy Blume and the "R" encyclopedia with its reproduction section. Then came the Internet. In the mid 1990s, school library media specialists began integrating Internet access into their programs. Soon students were at keyboards across the country finding information that reflected all aspects of our society. Some of this information was sexually explicit. Others discussed major issues of society including the environment, abortion, capital punishment, and political viewpoints. For the first time in the history of school libraries, resources that were not affirmatively selected by school librarians and other school personnel were placed in front of students. Software tools, commonly called filter programs, were created to block access to selected pieces of information on the Internet. Often this information deals with sex or a controversial issue such as witchcraft, religions, or societal problems. Librarians in all areas of the profession, including school library media centers, have had to do a great deal of soul-searching and research in order to create, implement, and live with Internet access for students.

A variety of Internet access policies are in place in school libraries. They include:

- Filtering every computer
- Filtering student computers but not adult computers
- Not filtering anyone

Because information that would be available is prevented from reaching patrons, intellectual freedom is compromised. School library media specialists in the pro-filter camp often claim that the breadth and depth of the information on the Internet far exceeds that which is reasonable to provide in a school setting. School library media specialists in the no-filter camp claim that students must learn how to handle the vast resources of the Internet and that filtering not only infringes their First Amendment rights but also prevents valuable education from taking place. The decision on filtering is often made by administrators, technical employees, and school library media specialists in light of specific school circumstances.

In December of 2000, then President Bill Clinton signed the Children's Internet Protection Act (CIPA) into law. This piece of legislation dictated that school districts who wish to receive federal funds from three sources — E-rate discounts for Internet access and service or internal network connections, funds from Title III of the Elementary and Secondary Education Act that are used to purchase computers to gain access to the Internet or to pay the direct costs associated with accessing the Internet, and state administered monies from the Library Service and Technology Act that fund access to the Internet — had to create an Internet use policy and had to use an Internet software filter (Gardner, 2002, 40). School library media specialists, upon accepting a position, must discover the route schools have taken with regard to CIPA regulations. Some districts have decided that the cost of complying with the legislation is too high and they have decided not to accept the affected federal funds. Other districts have decided to install a software filter. If this is the direction the district has taken, then school library media specialists have an ethical imperative to take the necessary steps to ensure that intellectual freedom is maintained at the highest possible level. These steps include lobbying for minimal filtering, educating the entire school community about the issues surrounding filtering, and providing access to filtered sites when they are necessary for the educational process.

Important Policies

Selection and reconsideration policies are crucial to every school library media program. Selection and reconsideration policies provide guidance to all school personnel — including school library media specialists — regarding why and how to select, de-select (weed), and reconsider resources. The policies also make a strong statement to every member of the community regarding how these processes take place. The school board should approve the policies. This provides both legal and political coverage for the school library media specialist and the school district.

Because of the importance of these policies, they should take into consideration the mission and vision of the school district as well as the mission and vision statements of the school library media program. The selection section should discuss why resources are provided and how those resources are selected. The same information regarding de-selecting resources is important to include. Criteria by which resources are withdrawn from the collection should be explicitly stated.

Because it is a rare school library media specialist who retires from the profession having never received a challenge to a resource, it is important that a reconsideration policy be created and approved by the school board. The policy should list the steps that the district will follow during the process of reconsidering a resource.

An Ounce of Prevention:
Promoting Intellectual Freedom

The best time to discuss intellectual freedom and its applicability in school library media centers is before a challenge happens. School library media specialists should educate everyone (teachers, students, administrators, school board members, and community members) about the benefits of upholding intellectual freedom. This education can take place via articles, lectures, discussion groups, displays, and a variety of other vehicles. In order for education about intellectual freedom to be successful, school library media specialists should:

- Choose an aspect of intellectual freedom to explore
- Decide on the population to educate about the specific aspect
- Select appropriate method(s) to deliver the message
- Deliver the message
- Evaluate the effectiveness of the program

Conclusion

The nature of intellectual freedom is such that it is easier to identify when it does not exist in a library than when it does. The ALA Intellectual Freedom manual states:

> Intellectual Freedom cannot bring itself into existence. Librarians must apply the principles of intellectual freedom to activities undertaken daily—materials selection, reference service, reevaluation, protection of confidential patron information, and most important, collection building. It is in acquisition and its product, the collection, that intellectual freedom must be reflected (ALA, 2002, xvii).

Works Cited

American Library Association. Office for Intellectual Freedom. (2002). *Intellectual Freedom Manual*, (6th edition). Chicago, IL: American Library Association.

Asheim, Lester. [n.d.] *Censorship vs. selection*. Retrieved September 10, 2002, from <www.informatics.buffalo.edu/faculty/ellison/Syllabi/580/NotCensor.html>.

Board of Education, Island Trees Union Free School District No. 26 v. Pico. 457 U.S. 853, 102 S.Ct. 2799, 73 L.Ed.2d 435. 1982.

Case v. Unified School District No. 233. 908 F. Supp. 864. 1995.

The Children's Defense Fund Web site. (2002) Retrieved September 2, 2002, from <http://www.children'sdefense.org/keyfacts.htm>.

Doyle, R. P. (2001) *The 2001 banned books resource guide*. Chicago, IL: American Library Association.

Gardner, C. (2001-2002) "To government regulations be true." *Educational Leadership*, 59(4), 40.

Maslow, A. (1999). *Toward a psychology of being*. New York: Wiley.

Newman, L. (1989). *Heather has two mommies*. New York: Alyson Wonderland.

Tinker v. Des Moines School District. 393 U.S. 503, 89 S.Ct. 733, 21 L.Ed.2d 731. 1969.

Todd v. Rochester Community Schools. 200 N.W.2d 90. MI. Ct. App. 1972.

Willhoite, M. (1989). *Daddy's roommate*. New York: Alyson Wonderland.

Discussion Questions

1. Your school is in a very conservative area. Your school offers a course in international politics. Part of the curriculum of that course is a study of the conflict in the Middle East. To support this unit, you purchase a book that explains the Middle East conflict from the Islamic viewpoint. A teacher in your school complains about the work, stating that it endorses terrorism and is therefore a violation of the USA Patriot Act. What is the appropriate response, according to the Code of Ethics?

2. Your school is in a very liberal and forward-thinking community. Families are quite diverse, with several gay couples among the school parents. The school board, however, is dominated by a conservative element. How do these considerations affect your collection development decisions and what resources will you use to defend your collection development policy?

3. Computerized reading incentive programs are popular in your district, and your principal has decided that one program is the solution to your school's poor reading scores on the high stakes test. Students will only be allowed to check out books that are within their tested reading levels, and all books will be marked with reading levels for ease of browsing. What ethical concepts come into play for the librarian?

4. The Internet presents an intellectual freedom dilemma. It provides access to much more information than libraries could ever afford to purchase, but it also provides access to inappropriate and even dangerous material. Describe the ethical dilemma this presents for the librarian, and enumerate the professional resources that reiterate the appropriate positions.

5. Selection and reconsideration are important concepts. Knowing that one might face forced reconsideration of materials may influence a librarian's selections. How does one plan for and avoid self-censorship (purchasing only those materials you know will not cause controversy)?

Chapter Seven
Ethics in Intellectual Property
By Carol Simpson

When one speaks of intellectual property, ethics frequently takes a backseat to law. Discussions of what is "right" may be entirely irrelevant because the decision is out of our hands. Federal (and sometimes state) law has established appropriate practice, and our impression of what is right, or fair, has absolutely nothing to do with what must happen in reality. For example, it is known that rewards work wonders for performance. Few things motivate students better than telling students there will be a desirable reward at the end of the work. A promise of a movie or other entertainment, however brief, can be a significant factor in getting students (especially elementary students) to complete work. The reward is the "right" thing to do for the education of the students. However, federal law states that such rewards are not permissible under the educational fair use exemptions of copyright law. These types of non-instructional performances must be licensed or otherwise paid for, while other school uses of video (direct teaching, for example) may be used freely and without charge. Is it a wonder why teachers, long indoctrinated to think FIRST of student achievement, frequently ignore the mandate of federal law?

Knowing the law, however, only makes one feel guilty when one knows that the interests of children will (and likely should) come first. To do what is right for the children may mean violating the law, and obeying the law may mean denying a student something he or she would use to enhance learning. It is an ethical dilemma. Those who own and control intellectual property contend that there is ample protection in the law to allow for educational uses of intellectual property. Most items used for direct instruction may be used under the fair use exemption to copyright law or the various associated guidelines developed by coalitions of content owners and content users and endorsed as fair and reasonable by the affected parties. Practitioners in the field, however, know that arbitrary limits (like a maximum of nine instances of multiple copying of print documents per term) will never meet the needs of information-hungry students, and financially strapped school districts cannot hope to purchase additional resources. Frequent reminders about copyright compliance by librarians can strain collegial relationships, yet keeping the teacher, the school, and the district out of legal trouble is laudable. What is a librarian to do?

The ALA Code of Ethics requires that librarians respect and observe restrictions on the intellectual property of others. The fourth item in the Code states: "We recognize and respect intellectual property rights" (1995). The Association for Educational Communications and Technology (AECT) Code of Ethics states: "Shall inform users of the stipulations and interpretations of the copyright law and other laws affecting the profession and encourage compliance" (2001). This statement is placed under the section of the code dealing with commitment to society, indicating the overarching importance respect for the property of others is given in the code. Indeed, respect for others, even others who are remote and unseen, is at the core of intellectual property compliance.

Beyond ethical codes and federal law, the most effective means of garnering compliance with copyright and other intellectual property issues is school board policy. The national government and its laws seem to be a long way away. However, school board policy is close and swiftly enforced. While one might have little fear of being reported to federal authorities for infringing copyright and a violation might never have any personal repercussions, a violation of school board policy is tied directly to employment. With reason, school personnel walk on tiptoes around issues that have significant liability with school board policy. The school board is likely to be vigilant regarding anything that might bring a suit against the district. Equal opportunity issues, Americans with Disabilities Act (ADA) compliance, and other federally overseen programs yield severe penalties when the requirements are violated so school boards build policies that ensure compliance. Intellectual property issues are also federal requirements with serious penalties. School boards have added copyright compliance to their repertoire of policies that can result in personnel censure if violated. So if good citizenship is not enough of a carrot to lead them to compliance, if federal sanctions aren't enough of a stick, then the fear of school board action for violating board policy may be the way to get school personnel (including librarians) to step up to the ethical plate and follow the law.

While copyright law and its many vagaries make compliance a difficult process, and lots of the requirements of the law are not in the complete best interest of students all the time, it is, in fact, the law of the land. Our ethical foundations require that we comply with the law. AECT's Code states: "Shall observe all laws relating to or affecting the profession ..." (2001). ALA's Code doesn't address laws in general, but it does go straight to the heart of intellectual property law: "We recognize and respect intellectual property rights" (1995). Even though the law and its associated guidelines do not hand over to schools all the materials they would like to use gratis, there are pluses and minuses for both copyright holders and copyright consumers. Traditional U.S. government teaches that one does not ignore laws with which one does not agree. One works, instead, to change the law.

The remainder of this chapter will address ethical dilemmas associated with copyright compliance in many forms. The author makes a baseline assumption of understanding copyright law and its implementation. Virtually all English-speaking countries (especially the United States, Canada, Great Britain, and Australia) have the same foundations of intellectual property protection. These discussions will apply to use of intellectual property in a generic sense and are not designed to educate the reader on specific aspects of copyright law in a given country. Specific legal examples are drawn from U.S. law and should be verified with legal experts in other countries. For a fundamental understanding of intellectual property in your own country, please see a basic treatment of copyright law or intellectual property law (which includes trademarks and patents as well as copyright).

Print

The foundation of any library, print is the primary medium with which librarians work. Ethical issues in dealing with the printed work of others come into play in several aspects of library work. Most often those situations arise when materials are duplicated or are used in a way that does not follow the requirements of copyright law. How does a librarian respond to these things in a manner that fulfills the ethical requirement to respect intellectual property?

Key to keeping the library and the school in copyright compliance on print issues, the librarian wants to keep reminders of copyright high in the minds of patrons. Reminder or warning notices on copy-enabled equipment, such as photocopiers, scanners, and fax machines, makes copyright a daily concept.

Audiovisuals

Modern libraries use media transparently. It is information that is the core concept, and the means of delivery are less important than the message delivered. Librarians are key to legal use of audiovisual materials in a school since most of the audiovisual software and equipment go through the library. A vigilant librarian can both facilitate appropriate use of audiovisual resources and can identify materials that need no special permissions to use.

Marking videos, for example, to identify those with public performance rights makes it a simple matter to find a compliant program to show to a group of students who must stay in from recess because of inclement weather or because a teacher has taken ill and the substitute hasn't arrived yet. The mere fact that the videos are marked draws daily attention to the copyright issue, heightening awareness by faculty about appropriate uses (Simpson, 1999).

Since audiovisual use is likely to be the one most significant copyright infringement problem in school, vigilant notice by the librarian can markedly reduce the risk of the school regarding infringement actions. Ethically, it would be appropriate to notify an administrator if the school were at risk of a citation for hazardous physical conditions or for a violation of one of the ADA requirements. Risk from copyright infringement action is no less worthy of notice. One would certainly be remiss (not to mention potentially liable) not to notify an administrator if a copyright infringement activity occurred within the school (Simpson, 2001, 10–11).

Periodicals

A significant portion of the world's information is transmitted via periodical literature. Periodicals have risen in cost over the last 20 years in amounts far exceeding book costs. Schools, ever watchful of budgets, request librarians to reduce periodical subscriptions or simply fail to increase periodical budgets to enable the same numbers of subscriptions. Librarians try to be creative in arranging to provide the same amount with fewer resources. Some librarians form consortia to share periodical subscriptions with neighboring schools or districts. While resource sharing is a long-standing practice, when it comes to periodicals, some restrictions apply.

The National Commission on New Technological Uses of Copyright Works (CONTU) developed a set of guidelines for sharing periodicals among libraries. Publishers felt it was unfair for one library to subscribe to a periodical and to provide copies for many institutions, but fair use would dictate that some use of the periodical beyond the subscribing library would be appropriate. While the scope of this chapter doesn't permit the extreme detail brought forth in the CONTU guidelines covering periodical copying for interlibrary loans (as well as other forms of interlibrary loan), it is important to understand that both legally and ethically the librarian must control the amount of institutional copies sent forth from a given periodical title (Simpson, 2001, 93–99).

Internet

Librarians share. It is a basic tenet of the profession. Those who gather all their materials onto the shelves and shoo patrons away from "my" books are looked at with derision by their peers. So why is anyone surprised that librarians want to share their materials with the world via the Internet?

One of the six basic rights of a copyright holder is that of distribution. The owner of a work may decide where and when the work will be offered. It's logical, from the librarian's and teacher's perspective, to want to put important works on the school's Web site so students working at home may have the same access as those who would be at school. Alas, when a work is put on the Internet, it has been distributed to the world.

The Digital Millennium Copyright Act provides some protections for schools that inadvertently post materials to the Web (United States, 2002). Such protection does not extend to materials intentionally posted on the Web, however. For materials posted as part of a regularly scheduled course, the TEACH act, signed into law in November 2002, may have some provisions that will apply to the proposed use. While TEACH provides many failsafe provisions for copyright-protected teaching materials on the Web, the requirements of the law are complex and detailed (ALA, 2002). A librarian has an ethical obligation to assess proposed uses of materials on the Web against these guidelines and to consult with administration and faculty who will be mounting materials to help them understand their legal (and ethical) requirements.

Plagiarism

Surprised to see this heading here? Why? Plagiarism is an ethical violation in many ways. Not only does it cheat the learner of a learning experience, it robs the true creator of the work who was plagiarized of credit for his or her creation. Plagiarism has deprived politicians of higher office, students of degrees, and authors of acknowledgment of hard work.

While ALA does not specifically address plagiarism in its Code of Ethics, AECT (2002) states: "… giving accurate credit to those whose work and ideas are associated with publishing in any form." The ethical principle is clear. The professional addresses issues of intellectual citation to provide credit for all material used from the works of others. This requirement only addresses our professional practice, but one would hope ethical behavior on the part of librarians would encourage similar behavior on the part of professional colleagues and students. Routinely seeing citations and attributions on library documents would give the expectation that this is standard intellectual practice. For more discussion on plagiarism, see "The Life We Lead" in the Appendix.

Accessibility

Nothing tugs at the heart of a schoolteacher like a student with special needs. You see a willing child struggling against immense odds, trying to learn, and trying to overcome an unfair cut of the deck. It is second nature to provide anything you can, any way you can, so that student can have every possible advantage. What items can you provide for a student to ease his or her already considerable burden?

Fortunately, federal law provides many options to use copyright protected materials under special exemptions for the blind and physically handicapped. The key to using those provisions, however, is to see that the necessary applications are made on behalf of the patron. The Library of Congress and various state libraries have established guidelines for services for those who are unable to use standard print materials. Those who qualify for services get special exemptions to transform materials to different formats to facilitate use by those with visual, auditory, and physical disabilities as well as free loan of the necessary equipment to use the adapted materials. However, there are specific rules for how those adaptive materials may be made and how they must be used (Simpson, 2001, 24).

Modeling copyright compliance is probably the greatest ethical challenge for librarians. With so many school personnel having no training in copyright, the librarian may be the only person in the building who understands both the legal and ethical aspects of this important issue. Some librarians—mostly long time classroom teachers—still have the classroom teacher mindset. Many of these (usually inexperienced) librarians view the copyright dilemma from the standpoint of expediency rather then ethical practice. Others ignore ethical practice in an effort to build support for a shaky library program. Knowing that helpful, supportive relationships promote education and collegiality, a librarian who straightforwardly models copyright compliance while providing compliance support for student and faculty activities will walk the high road of the profession and society.

Works Cited

American Library Association. (1995). *Code of ethics of the American Library Association*. Retrieved March 3, 2003, from <http://www.ala.org/alaorg/oif/ethics.html>.

American Library Association. *The Technology, Education, and Copyright Harmonization (TEACH) Act*. (2002). Retrieved March 3, 2003, from <http://www.ala.org/washoff/teach.html>.

Association for Educational Communications and Technology. (2002). *Section 3. A code of professional ethics.* Retrieved March 3, 2003, from <http://www.aect.org/Intranet/Publications/ethics/ethics03.html>.

Simpson, C. (2001). *Copyright for schools: a practical guide* (3rd edition). Worthington, OH: Linworth.

Simpson, C. (1999). "Managing copyright in schools." *Knowledge Quest,* 28(1): 18–22.

United States Copyright Office. (2002). *Designation of Agent to Receive Notifications of Claimed Infringement.* Retrieved on March 3, 2003, from <http://www.copyright.gov/onlinesp/>.

Discussion Questions

1. When school administrators model total disregard for copyright laws, how can ethical principles guide librarian practice?

2. Spreading the word about ethical and legal use of the works of others can make one a pariah. In the interest of collegiality, what steps should one take to meet legal obligations and still be considered a "team player"?

3. Convenience and budget are strong motivators, both for the librarian and teachers. Budget and test scores drive administrators. What reasons would cause any of these groups to follow ethical and legal procedures to deal with the intellectual property of others?

Chapter Eight
Ethics in the Administration of School Library Media Centers

By Nancy Everhart

Iews Fronts, a regular feature in *American Libraries*, reports monthly on both positive and negative media coverage of librarians. A recent issue furnished accounts of crimes—including stealing historical documents from archives, murdering a girlfriend, shooting a co-worker and then oneself, and selling donated books online and keeping the profits—each committed by a librarian or a former librarian (News Fronts, 2002). While news of serious crimes being committed by members of the profession exists, less has been written about simple lapses in ethical judgment. This is particularly true concerning discussion of the ethical aspects of administering a school library media program.

Administering a school library media program is a multi-dimensional enterprise. The school library media specialist as program administrator, one of four distinct roles identified in *Information Power: Building Partnerships for Learning*, performs the following tasks:

- The library media specialist works collaboratively with members of the learning community to define the policies of the library media program and to guide and direct all of the activities related to it.
- The library media specialist is confident of the importance of the effective use of information and information technology to students' personal and economic success in their future lives; the library media specialist is an advocate for the library media program and provides the knowledge, vision, and leadership to steer it creatively and energetically in the 21st century.
- The library media specialist is proficient in the management of staff, budgets, equipment, and facilities; the library media specialist plans, executes, and evaluates the program to ensure its quality at a general level and on a day-to-day basis (AASL/AECT, 1998, 5).

A school library media specialist is in a unique position in the sense that he or she is generally the only faculty member having extensive managerial responsibilities. The principal and teachers are mostly unaware of a school library media specialist's managerial tasks since they are performed "behind the scenes." Lack of awareness also stems from principals and teachers receiving little or no instruction about school library media centers in their preparation programs (Hartzell, 1997). Consequently, the school library media specialist can be placed in the position of self-monitoring ethical practices as well as educating colleagues as to why certain administrative decisions have been made.

One method of educating teachers, administrators, and others, recommended in *Information Power*, is to collaborate with them to develop and publicize policies and procedures for the school library media center that reflect legal guidelines and professional ethics (AASL/AECT, 1998). By working in partnership on policies in collection development, challenges to materials, discipline, acceptable use, circulation, and others, school library media specialists achieve several objectives:

- Assure that school library media centers' policies support other school policies.
- Demonstrate commitment of the school library media program to ethical practices.
- Model ethical and responsible use of information and information technology.

Ethical Guidelines for Managing School Libraries

Two professional organizations, the American Library Association (ALA) and the Association for Education Communications and Technology (AECT) have published codes of ethics supplying frameworks for ethical decision making in administering school library media programs (AECT, 2001; ALA, 1995). ALA's Code lists eight guidelines to guide the work of librarians and other information professionals. AECT categorizes 25 principles in the distinct areas of Commitment to the Individual, Commitment to Society, and Commitment to the Profession. To provide a structure for this chapter, tenets from both codes, relevant to administrative aspects of the school media program, will be used a guide for discussion.

Access and Service

> **ALA:** We provide the highest level of service to all library users through appropriate and usefully organized resources; equitable service policies; equitable access; and accurate, unbiased, and courteous responses to all requests.
>
> **AECT:** Shall encourage independent action in an individual's pursuit of learning and shall provide open access to knowledge regardless of delivery medium or varying points of view of the knowledge.
>
> Shall refrain from any behavior that would be judged to be discriminatory, harassing, insensitive, or offensive and, thus, is in conflict with valuing and promoting each individual's integrity, rights, and opportunity within a diverse profession and society.
>
> Shall guarantee to each individual the opportunity to participate in any appropriate program.

Equitable access in school library media programs denotes access to the school library facility as well as its resources and services. Each student, regardless of race, nationality, ethnicity, home language, socioeconomic status, age, religion, ability level, exceptionalities, physical challenges, sexual orientation, and gender—receives equitable opportunities (National Board for Professional Teaching Standards, 2001).

Access to the Facility

The entire school population must be given the opportunity to visit the school library media center. To achieve this, the school library media specialist should "encourage flexible access to the programs and services of the library media program by developing and implementing policies for scheduling, space management, and materials circulation that meet the needs of students, teachers, and other members of the learning community" (AASL/AECT, 1998, 87).

In the flexibly scheduled school library media program, there is an ethical obligation to plan that all students receive equal access to the school library media center. To succeed in this goal, principal support and encouragement for collaborative teaching is required because some teachers will resist bringing their students to the library media center (McGregor, 2002, 78). It may become easier for the school library media specialist to collaborate only with friends on the faculty, those teachers who approach him or her first, or teachers in subject areas where he or she feels knowledgeable. Ethically, the school library media specialist needs to get each teacher involved so all students will benefit. Doug Johnson asserts that this may be a difficult undertaking.

> I have never met a media specialist in a flex program that meets with every teacher on staff, let alone for an equal amount of time. Granted those students whose teacher is cooperative get a superior learning experience. But what about the kids whose teachers are so isolationist that they don't even get to the library for book checkout, let alone to learn media skills? Shouldn't we be asking: Do we give some kids great skills and other kids no skills, or do we give all kids the ability to learn some skills knowing that we could do better in an ideal world? (2001, 39).

The sheer physical size of the school library media center facility will also impact access and scheduling. If a facility is large, multiple classes, small groups, and individuals can be accommodated whether there is fixed or flexible scheduling. In smaller spaces, this is much more difficult. Possible solutions to facilitate access include carving out some room for individual students to work while a class is in session, sending materials to classrooms on carts, and implementing access before and after school hours.

Once students are through the door, a fundamental ethical practice is to accommodate them in a welcoming manner, showing no difference in how you speak to, include, or otherwise engage all learners (National Board for Professional Teaching Standards, 2001). Applying this might involve the following scenarios:

- Demonstrating as much enthusiasm for the reluctant reader as the gifted student.
- Tolerating non-traditional hairstyles, dress, body piercing, and tattoos.
- Developing a discipline code and enforcing it evenly and fairly.
- Adapting the facility for the physically handicapped and for students whose first language is not English.
- Staying current on community matters and educating yourself about students' cultures.
- Learning all students' names.
- Appearing accessible via smiling, eye contact, and positive body language.
- Being sensitive to different learning styles.
- Planning programming that reflects proportionally the interests of the school population.

The effective school library media program begins in an inviting, attractive school library media center that extends this welcoming climate to all the

programs and activities throughout the school (AASL/AECT, 1998, 88). Therefore, it is imperative that the facility not be used as a detention center and students should not be restricted from using it entirely because of misbehavior.

Access to Resources

Student access to resources is clarified in *Access to Resources* and *Services
in the School Library Media Program: An Interpretation of the Library Bill
of Rights* by the American Library Association (2000). Administrative decisions may impose barriers to the principles of intellectual freedom and to
access to diversity via a wide range of resources. Major barriers between
students and resources include but are not limited to: imposing age or grade
level restrictions on the use of resources, limiting the use of interlibrary loan
and access to electronic information, charging fees for information in specific formats, requiring permission from parents or teachers, establishing
restricted shelves or closed collections, and labeling (ALA, 2000).

Imposing age or grade level restrictions on the use of resources and
establishing restricted shelves or closed collections often occur in elementary
school library media centers. Due to the wide range of children's abilities in
an elementary setting, one may find the collection arranged into easy (picture
books), fiction, and nonfiction or even by grade level. Although arrangement
of books in this manner is not technically an unethical practice, limiting students to certain areas based on their ages or grade levels is. In a recent
lengthy discussion on the school library e-mail list, LM_NET, school library
media specialists justified restricting access for the following reasons:

- Kindergarten and first grade students pulling books off the
  shelves and throwing them on the floor or on tops of shelves.
- Not having time to reshelve things.
- Today's parents not wanting their children checking out books
  that are too hard for them.
- Not having help to supervise students while they select books.
- Children needing guidance in selection (Flack, 2002).

The lack of, or incomplete, cataloging of materials may also hinder
comprehensive access to them. When materials are not cataloged, access is
limited because patrons will be oblivious that certain materials exist when
searching the catalog. This is especially true of audiovisual materials.
School library media specialists regularly rationalize this behavior by citing
the limited availability of commercial processing for audiovisual materials,
they are protecting "expensive" teaching materials from students or they are

saying it takes too much time to catalog nonprint resources. It is also unethical practice to exclude materials from union or Web-based catalogs. By keeping materials hidden from outside users in this manner, school library media specialists may believe it shields them from censorship efforts by parents or other groups or from borrowing via interlibrary loan.

Limiting the use of interlibrary loan in schools could possibly take the form of limiting the service only to faculty, limiting the number of items per student per year or per class, limiting by format such as not requesting audiovisual or fiction materials, or limiting by sending requests for materials having to do with school assignments only.

Access to electronic information might also be limited to school-related assignments and research. Necessitating keyboarding skills or age requirements, or having a teacher or school library media specialist present while searching, also restricts access. The Children's Internet Protection Act (CIPA) requires the filtering or blocking of certain visual depictions and requires schools and libraries to adopt and implement an Internet safety policy and to operate "technology protection measures" (blocking and filtering) if they receive federal funds (ALA, 2002). Ethical breaches may transpire if one is overzealous in configuring filtering software.

The American Library Association opposes charging user fees for the provision of information by all libraries and information services that receive their major support from public funds (1993). All information resources that are provided directly or indirectly by the library, regardless of technology, format, or methods of delivery, should be readily, equally, and equitably accessible to all library users. In schools, some of these fees might consist of overdue fines, rental fees for audiovisual materials, and printing fees for computer workstations.

Requiring permission from parents or teachers potentially encompasses all of the aforementioned circumstances. Access to audiovisual materials, electronic information, controversial resources, or interlibrary loan are areas of the collection where school library media specialists might unethically ask students to provide consent from a higher authority. The phrase "Ask the Librarian" can appear on the catalog record or signage. However, school library media specialists should be aware of The Children's Online Privacy Protection Act (COPPA) enacted in 1998. The Act, enforced by the Federal Trade Commission, requires commercial Web site operators to get parental consent before collecting any personal information from kids under the age of 13. COPPA allows teachers to act on behalf of a parent during school activities online but does not require them to do so. That is, the law does not require teachers to make decisions about the collection of their students' personal information. One should check to see whether your school district has a policy about disclosing student information (Federal Trade Commission, 2002).

Labeling is "the practice of describing or designating materials by affixing a prejudicial label and/or segregating them by a prejudicial system" (ALA, 1990). In this context, the labeling refers to employing rating system labels as to age-appropriateness of materials that have controversial content. The practice of affixing reading or grade level labels to *Accelerated Reader*™ or *Reading Counts*™ materials could be construed to be ethically questionable — especially if the labels are used as a technique to restrict the access to these materials.

Management of Personnel

> **ALA:** We treat co-workers and other colleagues with respect, fairness and good faith, and advocate conditions of employment that safeguard the rights and welfare of all employees of our institutions.
>
> **AECT:** Shall make reasonable efforts to protect the individual from conditions harmful to health and safety, including harmful conditions caused by technology itself.
>
> Shall delegate assigned tasks to qualified personnel. Qualified personnel are those who have appropriate training or credentials and/or who can demonstrate competency in performing the task.

Clerks, aides, and volunteers — both parent and student — are the most widespread types of personnel that school library media specialists will find themselves supervising. Clerks and parents, uncertified personnel, should not be left to perform the administrative tasks delineated in the beginning of this chapter. An especially critical area is teaching and supervising of students. Parents and volunteers should never be left alone in the library media center with students because of legal, as well as ethical, liabilities.

In order to obtain the most qualified support personnel, school library media specialists need to be involved in the interviewing process. Once support staff is hired, school library media specialists are duty-bound to provide them with comprehensive training. All those who work in the school library media center, including students and volunteers, should be educated about student privacy and confidentiality as well as other issues discussed in this book. The school library media specialist must have the authority to dismiss, or to recommend for dismissal, all personnel who do not uphold ethical practices.

Students willing to volunteer their time and services should not be exploited. An effort must be made to provide them with work that is also a learning experience. Student safety is an utmost concern. Areas where problems could arise are having students move large pieces of equipment, lift heavy boxes, climb on high ladders, and work with electrical or sharp objects. In today's schools, there are more serious dangers. The most grue-some example is the Columbine tragedy in Littleton, Colorado (Kniffel, 1999). The school library media center was the center of brutal shootings by two students. Ultimately, 12 bodies were found there (including one student volunteer), and the facility was left in ruins. Because students were fright-ened to return to the crime scene, an entirely new library media center was built. Surely, the school library media specialists at Columbine High School have needed to remain highly sensitive to students.

Advancing Personal Interests; Professional Honesty

ALA: We do not advance private interests at the expense of library users, colleagues, or our employing institutions.

We distinguish between our personal convictions and professional duties and do not allow our personal beliefs to interfere with fair representa-tion of the aims of our institutions or the provision of access to their informa-tion resources.

AECT: Shall honestly represent the institution or organization with which that person is affiliated, and shall take adequate precautions to distinguish between personal and institutional or organizational views.

Shall represent accurately and truthfully the facts concerning educa-tional matters in direct and indirect public expressions.

Shall not use institutional or Associational privileges for private gain.

Shall accept no gratuities, gifts, or favors that might impair or appear to impair professional judgment, or offer any favor, service, or thing of value to obtain special advantage.

Shall engage in fair and equitable practices with those rendering serv-ice to the profession.

Shall conduct professional business through proper channels.

Personal vs. Private Interests

The greatest opportunity for advancing personal interests, convictions, and beliefs exists in the selection of materials for the library media center's col-lection. School library media specialists can potentially build a collection that only includes items that support their own personal beliefs. Likewise, they can avoid purchasing materials about issues they find offensive. Politics, offensive language, sexuality, sexual orientation, violence, religion, creationism, witchcraft and the occult, racism, and sexism are currently the most controversial of issues and are areas where most professionals have opinions, viewpoints, and values (Reichman, 2001).

One purpose of professional training, however, is to develop the ability to recognize and transcend personal bias. The professional should also know how to take into account and to work with community and parental concerns, while still maintaining a high tolerance for our national diversity. By contrast, the censor's judgment is that of the individual, and it is most frequently based on criteria that are inherently personal and often intolerant.

Where the censor seeks reason to *exclude* materials, those engaged in the process of selection look for ways to *include* the widest possible variety of textbooks, library materials, and curricular supplements within the context of a well-defined curriculum with clearly articulated goals. Censorship responds to diversity with suppression; the selection process seeks instead to familiarize students with the breadth of available images and information while simultaneously erecting essential guideposts for the development of truly independent thought (Reichman, 2001, 7).

The recommendations that appear in ALA's Code of Ethics regarding the separation of private citizen versus librarian resonate more intensely within the public library field than school media (1995). Nonetheless, certain scenarios may well apply:

- Negotiating a personal discount from a vendor by promising a lucrative school contract.
- Inappropriately portraying oneself in political, religious, or social arenas as a representative of the school or school library media profession.
- Utilizing nepotism.
- Extending the time spent at a professional conference for a personal vacation.

Casey discusses abuses of power such as "borrowing" library funds to cover personal bills, requesting sexual favors from subordinate staff members, running a business from the library, encouraging the donation of valuable books to the library by arranging for the potential donors to receive very "generous" appraisals of the value of those donations, and accepting personal help from staff. He laments, "As serious and clear-cut as these instances of malfeasance might seem, it is not impossible that the persons committing them proceeded either with the notion that they were taking proper advantage of a position of authority that they had earned and deserved, or that they were doing nothing terribly wrong. It might even be a matter of the culprit saying, 'I'm really underpaid and deserve to take these 'extras.' It is expected that allowances be made for persons at 'my level of responsibility' " (1998, 35).

Appropriation of Funds

When school library media specialists prepare budgets for the expenditure of funds, monies are appropriated in various categories, or lines, for books, supplies, periodicals computers, software, and so forth. It is ethical to spend only the funds that have been earmarked in specific categories and not to juggle the monies after the budget has been approved. This is especially critical when controlling grant funds. In addition, when applying for grants, honest representation for the need for funding as well as in all areas of the application is compulsory.

On occasion, an administrator will take liberties with the library's budget, placing the school library media specialist in an awkward position. A principal might divert library funds to another program. Alternatively, an administrator might never direct state or federal allocations to the library media program that is entitled to the monies. In these situations, the school library media specialist should seek advice from union or association representatives on how to proceed or should report the infraction to the funding source directly.

Fund Raising

Fund raising is another area where ethical dilemmas arise. Is it ethical, or even fair, for school principals to expect the school library media specialist to hold book fairs, bake sales, and car washes to raise funds for library materials? What about selling items to students in the library such as candy, pencils, pens, or book covers? An ethical decision needs to be made as to whether these items are there for the convenience of students, whether all students can afford them, or as in the case of candy, whether one is unfairly using students.

Free Material and Donations

Even many ostensibly "free" items pose ethical conflicts because they can impose advertising messages on a captive audience (Consumers Union, 1998). One of the most popular, The Channel One Network, provides free televisions for classrooms in exchange for requiring that all students watch a 12-minute news show each day which includes two minutes of commercials (Channel One News, 2002). Book Adventure is a free online reading comprehension program, similar to *Accelerated Reader*™ (Book Adventure Foundation, 2002). Commercial sponsors who donate free coupons support it. Other companies who target schools and whose products could find their way into the school library media center are:

- Cover Concepts Marketing Services, Inc. — free book covers plastered with ads.
- *Careers*, *High School Sports* and *GO!* — free magazines with advertising.
- Campbell's Soup — students bring in labels to earn computers and other equipment for the school.
- Corporate teaching materials, such posters, videos, books, pamphlets, and bookmarks emblazoned with logos (Consumers Union, 1998).

It is essential to consider the implications of using commercial materials with students since use often implies endorsement of the products advertised. This also applies to products given out as rewards or prizes.

Personal Use

The plethora of resources available in an average school library media center, combined with the freedom the school library media specialist has to control his or her own time, generate ample opportunities for ethical breaches of conduct. One common example is the school library media specialist who uses library funds to purchase materials for his or her personal use. A few books on deep-sea fishing or pottery may be appropriate, but lining the shelves with volume after volume when there is no curriculum need or student interest is inappropriate.

Likewise, using the library photocopier to run off invitations to a bridal shower or to make copies of your tax return without reimbursement crosses a line. Computers pose their own dilemmas. Surfing the Net to find a good hotel for your weekend trip, downloading and printing recipes, shopping, banking online, and sending personal e-mail, these activities — known as "cyberslacking" — decrease productivity and rob the school of professional time (Grasser, 2002). Employers have been cracking down on cyberslacking behavior using Internet monitoring software.

Excellence in the Profession

ALA: We strive for excellence in the profession by maintaining and enhancing our own knowledge and skills, by encouraging the professional development of co-workers, and by fostering the aspirations of potential members of the profession.

AECT: Shall strive continually to improve professional knowledge and skill and to make available to patrons and colleagues the benefit of that person's professional attainments.

Paramount to attaining excellence in the profession is the employment of certified, full-time school library media specialists in each school. White maintains the profession's greatest ethical shortcoming is in the way it treats itself (1991). "It [the library profession] fails to protect itself by letting others into it, either because of administrative pressures ... or because of the rationalizations that unqualified staff must be used because there is no money to hire qualified staff. Doctors would never do this. In the absence of physicians, what physicians are supposed to do does not get done, and so money is found for more physicians. The result is not worse medicine, it is better medicine. The result for librarians is worse libraries, and nobody else even knows!" (White, 1991, 41).

In light of the fact that certified school library media specialists are not legally required nationwide, current members of the profession have an ethical responsibility to monitor hiring practices in their immediate areas (Everhart, 2002). They should educate administrators and the public about the benefits of employing certified personnel in states where school library media specialists are not mandated. They should also report infractions to the proper authorities in those states where school library media specialists are mandated, but the mandate is not being followed.

In order to act ethically in a profession that is continually and rapidly evolving, it is imperative to stay at the forefront of developments. Laws, national and state guidelines, community standards, trends, technological advances, and more all impact on the ethical administration of the school library media program. What may be considered ethical practice today may not be appropriate in the future.

Works Cited

American Association of School Librarians and Association for Educational Communications and Technology. (1998). *Information Power: Building Partnerships for Learning.* Chicago, IL: ALA/AECT.

American Library Association. (1990). *Statement on labeling: an interpretation of the Library Bill of Rights.* Retrieved September 2002, from <http://www.ala.org/alaorg/oif/labeling.html>.

American Library Association. (1993). *Economic barriers to information access: An interpretation of the Library Bill of Rights.* Retrieved September 2002, from <http://www.ala.org/alaorg/oif/econ_bar.html>.

American Library Association. (1995). *Code of Ethics of the American Library Association.* Retrieved September 2002, from <http://www.ala.org/alaorg/oif/ethics.html>.

American Library Association. (2000). *Access to resources and services in the school library media program: an interpretation of the Library Bill of Rights.* Retrieved September 2002, from <http://www.ala.org/alaorg/oif/accmedia.html>.

American Library Association. (2002). *Questions and answers on Children's Internet Protection legislation.* Retrieved September 2002, from <http://www.ala.org/cipa/q&a.html>.

Association for Educational Communications and Technology. (2001). *AECT: Code of ethics.* Retrieved September 2002, from <http://www.aect.org/About/Ethics.htm>.

Book Adventure Foundation. (2002). *Book adventure.* Retrieved September 2002, from <http://www.bookadventure.org/>.

Casey, J. B. (1998). *Ethics: It isn't just presidents who get in trouble!* American Libraries. 29, 35.

Channel One News. (2002). *About Channel One.* Retrieved September 2002, from <http://www.channeloneteacher.com/about/index.html>.

Consumers Union. (1998). "In-school promotion." *Selling America's kids: commercial pressures on kids of the 90s.* Retrieved September 3, 2002, from <http://www.consumersunion.org/other/sellingkids/inschoolpromo.htm>.

Everhart, N. (2002). "Filling the void." *School Library Journal,* 48(6), 44–49.

Federal Trade Commission. (2002). *Kidz privacy: For teachers.* Retrieved September 2002, from <http://www.ftc.gov/bcp/conline/edcams/kidzprivacy/teachers.htm>.

Flack, N. (2002). *Hit: Restricting areas of the library.* Retrieved September 2002, from <http://www.askeric.org/Virtual/Listserv_Archives/LM_NET/Current/msg00001.html>.

Grasser K. (2002). "Researchers find cyber-slacking abounds." *This is Carleton.* Retrieved September 2002, from <http://www.carleton.ca/duc/tic/02/feb11/article11.htm>.

Hartzell, G. N. (1997). "The invisible school librarian." *School Library Journal,* 43, 24–29.

Johnson, D. (2001). "It's good to be inflexible." *School Library Journal,* 47(11), 39.

Kniffel, L. (1999). "Murder rampage culminates in Colorado high school library." *American Libraries,* 30, 26–28.

McGregor, J. H. (2002). "Flexible scheduling: How does a principal facilitate implementation?" *School Libraries Worldwide*. 8, 71–84.

National Board for Professional Teaching Standards. (2001). Standard IX: Ethics, equity, and diversity. *Library media standards*. Retrieved September 2002, from <http://new.nbpts.org/standards/complete/ecya_lm.pdf>.

News fronts. (2002). *American Libraries*. 33, 13–29.

Reichman, H. (2001). *Censorship and selection: issues and answers for schools*. (3rd edition). Chicago: American Library Association.

White, H. S. (1991). "Teaching professional ethics to students of library and information science." *Ethics and the Librarian*, 31–43.

Discussion Questions

1. Teachers in a building have decided that, for the purposes of increasing student achievement on standardized tests, they want to rearrange the library by reading levels. Each of the levels will have a different colored stripe on the spine, and students will only be allowed to check out books on their tested reading level. What ethical considerations must the librarian evaluate before endorsing or rejecting this plan?

2. A new librarian has followed a long-loved one into a school with a difficult faculty. To make friends, the librarian plans to find out what each teacher's pet topics are and to stock up on new materials in those areas. One teacher is a quilter; another loves exotic cooking. To shore up relationships with those teachers, the new book order has several books on those topics. What ethical considerations apply here?

3. One teacher in a building tries to be supportive of the library program by not allowing her students to come to the library if the class has been rowdy. What ethical concepts are affected by this action, and how should the librarian react to be consistent with the Codes of Ethics?

4. What management practices are the most difficult to reconcile to the Codes of Ethics? Why?

Chapter Nine
Ethics in Internet Use
By Nancy Willard

Introduction

The Internet has emerged in the last decade as an extremely important conduit for information and communications. The vast majority of U.S. public schools are connected to the Internet. In 2001, an estimated 99% of U.S. public schools and 87% of instructional rooms had Internet access (U.S. Dept. of Ed., 2002). The school library is generally the first location within a school to have Internet access. Within the library, students have the opportunity to engage in self-exploration and discovery of information on the Internet. This raises concerns regarding the types of materials they may be accessing and how best to manage this access.

The objective of schools is to prepare students for active and effective participation in society. The information and communication resources of the Internet have become an essential component of this preparation. Schools are uniquely positioned to serve as the primary vehicle through which young people can develop the knowledge, skills, and motivation to use the Internet in a safe, a responsible, and an effective manner.

This chapter will discuss several legal and ethical issues that may arise related to the provision of Internet access in school libraries. Some of the issues discussed will be issues that are governed by policies or regulations that have been developed at a district or school level. The role of the school librarian will be to act in accord with the provisions of such policies and regulations. However, this chapter will take a broader perspective of the role of the school librarian than simply following district policies and regulations. A school librarian is an information specialist who others will and should look to for input and guidance on the development and implementation of such policies and regulations. In other words, this chapter envisions the role of a school librarian as a leader in ensuring the adequacy and appropriateness of the district's policies and regulations related to student and staff use of the Internet.

Protecting Young People by Preparing Them

In May 2002, the National Research Council (NRC) issued a report entitled *Youth Pornography and the Internet* (NRC, 2002). This report was the result of an intensive study of issues related to the concerns of youth access to inappropriate materials on the Internet. The report is an excellent resource for school librarians on these issues. The NRC report noted that much of the focus of attention to address Internet concerns has been on technology solutions.

Much of the debate about "pornography on the Internet" focuses on the advantages and disadvantages of technical and public policy solutions. Technology solutions seem to offer quick and inexpensive fixes that allow adult caregivers to believe that the problem has been addressed, and it is tempting to believe that the use of technology can drastically reduce or eliminate the need for human supervision. Public policy approaches promise to eliminate the sources of the problem.

In the committee's view, this focus is misguided: neither technology nor public policy alone can provide a complete—or even a nearly complete—solution. As a rule, public policy aimed at eliminating sources of sexually explicit material can affect only indigenous domestic sources, and a substantial fraction of such material originates overseas. Technology is also not a substitute for education, responsible adult supervision, and ethical Internet use.

For these reasons, the most important finding of the committee is that developing in children and youth an ethic of responsible choice and skilled for appropriate behavior is foundational for all efforts to protect them (NRC, 2002, 364–365).

The material set forth in this chapter is directed at the kinds of policy and educational strategies that are necessary to adequately protect students by preparing them to use the Internet in a safe and responsible manner. As information specialists, it is important for school librarians to understand and be effective advocates for best practices in this area.

Children's Internet Protection Act

In December 2000, Congress enacted the Children's Internet Protection Act (CIPA) (*42 U.S.C. 254*). This statute was enacted due to concerns about the presence of materials on the Internet that are considered inappropriate and potentially harmful for young people to access. CIPA raises issues related to the access of potentially harmful material, to approaches to protect against such access, and to student privacy related to Internet use.

CIPA requires that schools (and public libraries) receiving federal funds for technology abide by certain requirements. The basic requirements of CIPA for public schools are:

1. Enforce a policy of Internet safety for minors that includes monitoring the online activities of minors and the operation of a technology protection measure that protects against access to visual depictions that are obscene, child pornography, or harmful to minors [*47 U.S.C. 254(h)(5)(B)*].

2. Enforce a policy of Internet safety with respect to adults that includes the operation of a technology protection measure that protects against access to visual depictions that are obscene or child pornography [*47 U.S.C. 254(h)(5)(C)*].

3. Adopt an Internet safety plan that addresses the following elements:
   a. Access by minors to inappropriate matter on the Internet and World Wide Web.
   b. Safety and security of minors when using electronic mail, chat rooms, and other forms of direct electronic communications.
   c. Unauthorized online access by minors, including "hacking" and other unlawful activities.
   d. Unauthorized disclosure, use, and dissemination of personal information regarding minors.
   e. Measures designed to restrict minors' access to materials harmful to minors [*47 U.S.C. 254(l)(1)(A)*].

4. Provide public notice and hold a public hearing regarding the Internet safety plan [*47 U.S.C. 254(h)(5)(A)(iii)*].

The public library portions of CIPA were challenged in a case filed by the American Library Association and the American Civil Liberties Union (ALA). In late May 2002, the U.S. District Court held these provisions to be unconstitutional. As of the writing of this chapter, the ruling is on appeal to the U.S. Supreme Court.

Use of Commercial Filtering Software in Public Schools

Questions Regarding Constitutionality

In the ALA case, the court ruled that CIPA was unconstitutional in the case of public libraries because the actions required under the law would violate the constitutional rights of library patrons—adults and minors—to access constitutionally protected material on the Internet (*Id* at *102a*)[1]. The court considered access to the Internet in public libraries to be so intrinsically linked to basic First Amendment values, that it applied the strictest level of scrutiny to the restriction placed on its use by filtering software (*Id* at *128a*). Although there was a compelling interest in protecting children and adults from accidental or intentional access to inappropriate material, commercial filtering systems are not narrowly tailored to address this concern because they block access to substantial amounts of material that are constitutionally protected (*Id* at *139a* and *148–9a*). Additionally, the court found that there were less restrictive alternatives that can be used to address the concerns (*Id* at *157–67a*). The ability to override the filter to provide access does not cure the constitutional deficiency (*Id* at *167–177a*).

The ruling in *ALA* is not directly applicable to the situation of the use of commercial filtering software in schools. It is probable, given the environment of schools, that the standard of analysis that will be applied will be that such use must be reasonably related to legitimate pedagogical concerns and not result in viewpoint discrimination (*see Board of Education, Island Trees Union Free School District No. 26 v Pico, 457 US 853, 1982*). However, the findings and analysis of the ALA case provide important insight into the question of the constitutionality and ethics of using commercial filtering software in schools.

Courts generally grant significant deference to the authority of school officials to make decisions for their local school communities. This deference is grounded in the perspective that the business of school is conducted

---

[1] In ALA, the issue before the court was the constitutionality of CIPA. When courts consider the constitutionality of a federal requirement that is tied to funding, they use a four-part analysis that was first enunciated in *South Dakota v. Dole, 483 U.S. 203* (1987). Only one part of this analysis was relevant in the case—that was the question of whether CIPA requires libraries to violate the constitutional rights of their patrons. Therefore, it was necessary to consider whether the use of filtering violated the constitutional right of free speech of library patrons. For this reason, the ruling can provide insight into the issue that the use of filtering in schools violates the constitutional rights of students.

in an open environment, where information about how decisions are made is readily available, and that school officials can be held publicly accountable to their local community for their decisions (*Pico* at 863).

When school officials delegate authority to commercial filtering software companies that protect their processes as proprietary-protected confidential information to make the determinations of what material students can and cannot access on the Internet, there is no access to information about how such decisions are made and there is no public accountability on the part of the company for such decisions. Such delegation of authority is made under the following conditions:

- Professional educators or librarians are not making blocking decisions.
- Category definitions and categorization decisions of the companies are made without reference to *local* community or school standards.
- Lists of blocked sites as well as the specific methods that filtering software companies use to compile and categorize lists, including search/block keywords and blocking processes, are considered confidential information and are not disclosed to school officials.
- There is no vehicle to ensure public accountability on the part of the commercial filtering software companies. Such companies are not subject to freedom of information/access to public records laws. Their boards of directors cannot be held accountable to the citizens of a community through an election process.
- Filtering companies also sell their products to other customers, including government agencies, companies, restrictive governments, and conservative religious organizations. It is unknown how the existence of such other markets may impact the blocking decision making of these companies.

Under such circumstances, the delegation of authority and abdication of responsibility by school officials will likely not be considered to be reasonably related to legitimate pedagogical concerns. This is especially true in light of the conclusions in the NRC report regarding the concerns of inappropriate reliance on technology quick fix solutions, rather than a strong focus on education and supervision. What the court in *ALA* considered "less restrictive alternatives," are, in the eyes of the NRC, the foundation of an appropriate response to the concerns.

Further, there is ample evidence from multiple sources that commercial filtering software restricts student access to materials based on inappropriate viewpoint discrimination. In some cases, such viewpoint discrimination is evident on its face—the inclusion of information related to sexual orientation in the same category as sexual technique and swinging or the inclusion of non-traditional religious topics in the same category as Satanism. The companies may also engage in intentional viewpoint discrimination that would not be detectable without full and complete access to information the companies protect as proprietary. For example, blocking access to sites addressing safe sex or homosexuality in the pornography-related categories or blocking access to political protest sites in categories such as "anarchy" or "violence." It is highly likely that over zealousness and a desire to err on the side of caution on the part of employees who are making blocking decisions is resulting in the prevention of access to material based on viewpoint discrimination. This issue is discussed more below.

The court in *ALA* determined that the ability of librarians to override the filter did not cure the constitutional deficiencies (*Id* at *167–177a*). It is reasonable to presume that the fact that school officials can override the filter to provide access to inappropriately blocked sites would not cure the constitutional deficiencies related to the use of these products in public schools. Given the excessive demands placed on technology staff in schools, it is simply not possible to override the filter to provide access to desired appropriate information in a timely manner. Further, students are likely to be reticent to request access to inappropriately blocked material that is controversial or sensitive in nature. Students simply do not request that the filter be overridden because they know that they can more rapidly access such material through their unfiltered Internet access at home. The students who do not have home access are placed at a significant disadvantage.

The question of the constitutionality of CIPA is less clear. If CIPA is construed to require the use of commercial filtering software, then it is likely to be considered unconstitutional. If the requirements of CIPA are construed more liberally—to encompass the use of technologies that do not require the delegation of authority to companies that cannot be held publicly accountable—then CIPA may be considered constitutional. It appears to be possible to comply with the provisions of CIPA by using "technology protection measures" other than commercial filtering software. The NRC report contains a chapter that discusses various protective technologies that could be considered for use in public schools to comply with the CIPA requirements (NRC, 2002, 267–326).

Research on the Effectiveness of Commercial Filtering Software

A study conducted by the Family Foundation reviewed the effectiveness of filtering software in blocking access to pornography and allowing for access to health information sites (Rideout, et al., 2002). Kaiser researchers evaluated the six top-selling filtering software products in schools plus AOL Parental Controls. The filters were set at three different configurations: Least Restrictive — blocking only the pornography-related category or categories; Intermediate Restrictive — blocking those categories that are most likely to be considered inappropriate in a school setting; and Most Restrictive — blocking all categories conceivable in a library or school setting. Based on the author's informal conversations with school personnel, a reasonable assumption is that most public schools have configured their filtering systems at or above the Intermediate Restrictive level.

Kaiser researchers tested the filtering systems' abilities to block access to pornography under conditions simulating intentional access and accidental access. To assess intentional access, they conducted searches on terms likely to lead to pornography. To assess accidental access, they attempted to access the pornography sites that appeared in the search results when they were seeking appropriate health information. To assess intentional access, they conducted searches on terms likely to reveal pornography sites, such as XXX.

Under conditions simulating intentional access, one in 10 sites containing pornography was accessible. This failure rate was consistent across the blocking configurations (Least — 87% of pornography sites blocked; Intermediate — 90% of pornography sites blocked; Most — 91% of pornography sites blocked) (NRC, 2002, 256–257).

Under conditions simulating accidental access, the filters allowed access to pornography 38% of the time — one in three times when set at the Least Restrictive configuration. The results for the other levels of configuration were not reported (NRC, 2002, 256–257).

The Kaiser study also assessed the ability to access sites containing health information across a broad range of topics. These topics included health topics unrelated to sex, health topics related to sexual body parts, health topics related to sex, and sites presenting potentially controversial health information.

A close analysis of the data reveals blocking patterns that present significant concerns of viewpoint discrimination. While at the least restrictive level only 1.4% of all health information sites were blocked, roughly 10% of health information sites related to "safe sex," "condoms," and "gay" were blocked.

At the intermediate and most restrictive levels in those categories where the subject area is controversial, the rate of overblocking was significantly higher. At the intermediate restriction level, typical of most school settings, the filters blocked potentially controversial health information sites at the following levels: ecstasy (drug education sites)—24.9%, safe sex—20.5%, condoms—27.7%, gay—24.6%, and lesbian—17.1%. At the most restrictive level, which includes categories that some districts may be blocking, the filters blocked potentially controversial health information sites at the following level: ecstasy (drug education sites)—36.2%, safe sex—50.0%, condoms—55.4%, pregnancy—31.6%, birth control—34.7%, abortion—44.6%, gay—59.9%, and lesbian—59.0% (reporting only those categories with blocking rates over 30%) (10).

The Kaiser study demonstrated the failures of filtering in preventing access to inappropriate material as well as in overblocking potentially controversial information. In assessing library policies and practices, librarians should consider how long it might take for a student at an unsupervised computer to test 10 pornography sites to find the one unblocked site. As it also appears that filters will not prevent accidental access of inappropriate material, librarians should consider what other actions should be taken to protect younger students and educate older students about how to avoid accidental access. The prevention of student access to appropriate material by filters should also be of concern to librarians.

Implications for Librarians

Decisions about filtering software are made at the district level and, occasionally, at the school level. Potentially, decisions about filtering levels may be made at the building level. Therefore, the only role that the school librarian will most likely play will be to seek to influence this decision making by providing data and arguments that will encourage the district to make the best choices. Actions that may be successful in influencing policy and that may help to protect students may include:

- Encourage the use of alternative technology protection measures that can meet CIPA requirements without the loss of local accountability and control.
- If the district is committed to using filtering software, encourage that such software be configured at the least restrictive level and request authorization for the ability to override, review, and provide students with access to sites that have been inappropriately blocked by the filtering software.
- Encourage students and teachers to report any instances where they believe they have been blocked from accessing appropriate sites in the course of conducting educationally related research. Provide this data to district decision makers. Librarians could

also request access to the blocked URL reports to evaluate the degree to which students are being prevented from accessing appropriate sites and are seeking access to inappropriate sites.

■ Recognize that filtering software will not protect against accidental access to inappropriate material. Librarians should provide instruction to students regarding how to avoid accidentally accessing inappropriate material and what to do if they have gotten to such material. Students should be instructed to turn off the monitor and call a teacher or adult lab monitor. The teacher or adult lab monitor can then backtrack to determine how the student accidentally got to the wrong site. This insight can assist in providing better instruction to students.

■ Recognizing that filtering software will not protect against intentional access to inappropriate material, ensure that the library has established appropriate supervision and monitoring policies and practices to detect instances of intentional student misuse. The material that follows offers a more extensive discussion of supervision and monitoring.

Social and Educational Strategies to Address Internet Use Concerns

There is a growing recognition of the fact that it is simply not possible to protect children with technological tools that are neither infallible, nor present on every Internet access device. Filtering software does not address all of the issues of concern when students are using the Internet at school either.

NRC Findings

The NRC report outlined social and educational strategies that are considered foundational to protecting children. The following are the findings and observations about social and educational strategies contained in the NRC report (256–257):

1. Social and educational strategies directly address the nurturing of character and the development of responsible choice. Because such strategies locate control in the hands of the youth targeted, children may make mistakes as they learn to internalize the object of these lessons. However, explaining why certain actions were mistaken will help children learn the lessons that parents and other adults hope they will learn.

2. Though education is difficult and time consuming, many aspects of Internet safety education have been successful in the past several years. While it is true that Internet safety education, acceptable use policies, and even parental guidance and counseling are unlikely to change the desires of many adolescents to seek out sexually explicit materials, parents are more aware of some of the other dangers (such as meeting strangers face-to-face) and know more about how to protect their kids better than ever before. (This is true even though more needs to be done in this area.) Children are better educated about how to sense whether the person on the other end of an instant message is "for real." Many of them have developed strategies for coping, and children with such strategies increasingly understand the rules of the game better than their parents. Little of this was true five years ago.

3. Social and educational strategies are generally not inexpensive, but they require tending and implementation. Adults must be taught to teach children how to make good choices in this area. They must be willing to engage in sometimes-difficult conversations. In addition, social and educational strategies do not provide a quick fix with a high degree of immediate protection. Nevertheless, they are the only approach through which ethics of responsible behavior can be cultivated and ways of coping with inappropriate material and experiences can be taught.

4. Social and educational strategies have relevance and applicability far beyond the limited question of "protecting kids from porn on the Internet." For example, social and educational strategies are relevant to teaching children to:
   - Think critically about all kinds of media messages, including those associated with hate, racism, senseless violence, and so on;
   - Conduct effective Internet searches for information and navigate with confidence;
   - Evaluate the credibility and motivation of the sources of the messages that they receive;
   - Better recognize dangerous situations on the Internet;
   - Make ethical and responsible choices about Internet behavior—and about non-Internet behavior as well; and
   - Cope better with exposure to upsetting and disturbing experiences and material found on the Internet (256–257).

A Comprehensive Education and Supervision-Based Approach

As information specialists, librarians can advocate for a more comprehensive approach to addressing concerns related to the Internet. The following are recommendations for key components of a comprehensive approach. This approach will need to be integrated into district policies and regulations related to Internet use.

- Place a strong focus on the effective educational use of the Internet. When students are actively engaged in exciting Internet learning, the opportunities and inclinations for misuse are significantly reduced. The foundation for this strong educational focus is professional development and curriculum development.
- Enact a comprehensive Internet use policy that addresses issues related to the use of the Internet and provides the foundation for an educational program addressing the safe and responsible use of the Internet. This policy should address access to inappropriate Internet material by students and staff, the safety and security of students when using electronic communication, misuse, and illegal use of the Internet including copyright, plagiarism, harmful speech, and computer security, and the unauthorized disclosure of personal information of students.
- Follow a strategy that reflects an understanding of the age and understandings of the students. The focus for elementary students should be on limiting access to safe Internet places for accessing information and communicating. Elementary students do not have the knowledge or skills to adequately protect themselves on the open Internet. By middle school, the strategy should shift. Students of this age are freely using the Internet from a variety of locations. The focus should be on comprehensive education and effective supervision and monitoring that is sufficient to detect and respond to instances of misuse.
- Provide comprehensive education to staff, students, and parents regarding safe and responsible Internet use issues and skills, as appropriate to their ages and understanding. This education should prepare students to independently protect their personal safety when using the Internet, to respond effectively to Internet concerns, and to abide by their responsibilities as "cybercitizens." Incorporate Internet safety issues into other curriculum areas, such as addressing online predation in sex education classes.

- Develop or utilize an educational Web site that channels student use to sites that have been reviewed by educators, librarians, and other professionals and that have been determined to present accurate, educationally relevant information in an appropriate manner. Limit elementary student access to these pre-reviewed educationally appropriate sites unless the teacher is closely supervising them. Direct or channel secondary students to such sites, while allowing for open access when necessary and appropriate.
- Establish a safe electronic communication system that promotes communication for educational purposes only.
- Establish supervision and monitoring systems that ensure accountability. Students and staff should know that they have limited privacy in their Internet use through the school system. Offer parents the ability to access to the Internet records of their children so that they can assure themselves that their children are using the Internet at school in accord with their family values.
- Respond with appropriate discipline in the event of misuse, using such instances as "teachable moments." Additionally, review instances of misuse to reevaluate the district's approach. Schools should not overreact and impose excessive discipline in cases of student misuse of the Internet. Looking at a pornography site on the Internet should not be treated more seriously than looking at a *Playboy* in the locker room. Harassment is harassment, whether it occurs online or in person. The focus of the discipline should be the inappropriateness of the act, not the medium by which the act was accomplished. Schools should also be very careful not to punish students for making a mistake when they use the Internet. Excessive punishment and inappropriately applied punishment is not only unfair, but it will create a situation where students will be reticent to approach an adult if they have gotten into a situation on the Internet that has made them uncomfortable or could present danger to their safety.
- Use a variety of technologies to support this comprehensive approach, including technologies that block access to sites that have rated themselves as sexually explicit or inappropriate for minors, technologies that limit or guide students to educationally appropriate sites, technologies that protect against unwanted commercial or pornographic electronic communication, and technologies that facilitate effective monitoring of student use.

Strategies for School Librarians

As is evident from both the presentation of social and educational strategies by the NRC and the recommendations for a comprehensive approach to addressing the safe and responsible use of the Internet, there is much work for library professionals in this effort. Specific strategies that a school librarian can implement that will help to promote the safe and responsible use of the Internet include:

- Promote high quality educational use of the Internet in the library. Establish library policies that restrict or limit non-educational use, including policies that allow students seeking computer/Internet access for class-related purposes to have priority access over other uses.
- Maintain data regarding how the Internet is being used in the library. Such data will provide critically important insight on the degree to which the district has engaged in the activities necessary to support quality educational use. If the library's computers are not being effectively used by students for educational activities, this provides a clear indication of the need for the district to enhance its activities in professional development and curriculum development.
- Promote the establishment of a district Web site that provides access to pre-reviewed educational materials. Ensure that such a Web site provides access to a broad range of quality materials, including materials that some would consider controversial, much in the same way a library collection is developed to represent all points of view. Assist teachers in learning how to develop their own class or lesson Web pages.
- Provide education related to safe and responsible use of the Internet and media literacy. School librarians can champion the need for such instruction and may be the most appropriate staff member to deliver such instruction[2]. The box on page 142 contains a recommended list of safe and responsible use issues that should be addressed through education.

---

[2] The author of this article is also the author of a book that addresses these issues. *Computer Ethics, Etiquette, and Safety for the 21st Century Student* is available through the International Society for Technology in Education <http://www.iste.org>.

Outline of Safe and Responsible Use Issues

The following is a recommended outline of issues related to the safe and responsible use of the Internet. An overarching instructional focus should be on media and information literacy, which will provide an important foundation for the following topics.

- Avoiding unintentional access — effective search skills, URL porn-napping.
- Dealing with accidental access — getting out of mouse-traps, reporting.
- Recognizing and dealing with unwanted SPAM.
- Communication safety skills — protection of privacy, recognizing predators, reporting predators, protecting friends.
- Protection of privacy — personal privacy, privacy of others, privacy on commercial sites, profiling.
- Harmful speech — defamation, harassment, violation of privacy, abusive language, flame wars, etiquette, recognizing harmful speech/hate sites, consequences for offenders, effective victim responses.
- Responsible speech — free speech rights, effective online advocacy, disability IT access.
- Copyright — rights and responsibilities.
- Plagiarism.
- Computer security — unlawful computer activities.
- Network security and resource limits — passwords, viruses, quotas, downloads, group lists.
- Online addiction — sexual, violent games, gambling, just wasting time, other.

Supervision, Monitoring, and Privacy Concerns

Under CIPA, districts must certify that they enforce a policy that includes monitoring the online activities of students [*47 U.S.C. 254 (h)(5)(B)*]. The term "monitoring" is not defined. Monitoring activities could include real-time staff supervision, the use of technologies for real-time remote monitoring of computer screens, and the review of Internet use records. Some newer technologies are able to monitor use of the Internet and report on use that appears to be in violation of policy.

However, such monitoring will raise concerns regarding student privacy. The policies of the American Library Association and the American Association of School Librarians both reinforce the importance of respecting the privacy of patrons in their selection of reading materials (AASL, 1999).

Student use of the Internet raises concerns that challenge this underlying interest in respecting privacy. When students read materials that have been placed in a school library, they are reading material that has already been pre-reviewed by librarians. Such material has been determined to present accurate information, to present information an appropriate manner, and to be appropriate for the age level of the students. Such is clearly not the case with respect to material students may access on the Internet.

Sometimes educators and librarians express support for the use of filtering software in the context of addressing privacy concerns. The argument presented is that since filtering software protects against access to inappropriate material, this relieves the staff of the obligations of supervision and thereby protects the privacy of students. This argument is weakened by data suggesting that one in 10 pornography sites is accessible even with filtering and that filtering software is preventing access to potentially controversial information.

Virtually all districts have decided that student use of the Internet simply must be supervised and monitored; therefore, this is not a decision that a school librarian will be able to change. Such supervision and monitoring will necessarily interfere with a student's privacy. In some districts, there is an express standard that students should expect "no privacy" when using the Internet and a requirement that all student use of the Internet be supervised by school staff. Other districts provide for "limited privacy," noting that student use will be supervised and monitored and setting forth information on how and when individualized searches will be conducted. The latter approach is preferred, and school librarians may be able to influence policies and practices in this regard.

Legal Standards

Monitoring student and staff use of the Internet in schools necessarily raises the issue of legal standards related to student and staff privacy. Most of the case law related to privacy issues has emerged in the context of criminal cases and has related to an interpretation of the Fourth Amendment restrictions on search and seizure. This case law has also been interpreted in the context of searches of student or staff personal belongings in school.

The initial analysis in such cases relates to the degree to which privacy is "expected." The United States Supreme Court in *Katz v. United States, 389 U.S. 347* (1967), first enunciated the constitutional standards related to expectations of privacy and established a two-part test. The first part of the test requires "[t] he person must have had an actual or subjective expectation of privacy" (*Id.* at *350–52, 360*). The second part requires that this subjective "expectation be one that society is prepared to recognize as 'reasonable' " [*Id.* at *361* (Harlan, J., concurring)]. If these two tests are satisfied, then there is said to be a reasonable expectation of privacy.

Two additional doctrines that have emerged in this area appear to be relevant. The first is the "plain view" doctrine. Under the plain view doctrine, if a public official, who is legitimately where he or she is able to be, sees something in plain view, there are no privacy protections (*Hester v. United States, 265 U.S. 57* (1924)). Students using the Internet at computers in a school computer lab or the library, where the screen is plainly visible, are using the Internet in "plain view" and should have no expectations of privacy.

The second doctrine is that of consent. In *United States v. Simons, 206 F.3d 392, 398* (4th Cir. 2000), a government agency network services administrator found patterns of use that indicated that an employee was accessing Internet pornographic material. Further search was made of the employee's computer and a significant number of pornographic files were found. The employee objected to the search on Fourth Amendment grounds. The court upheld the search, indicating that the government agency's policy on computer use indicated the potential of audits of Web usage to identify instances of inappropriate activity.

Does this mean that there should be no expectation whatsoever of privacy for students (or staff) when they are using the Internet? Imagine a district or school policy with a "no privacy" standard that has elaborated on that policy by saying "Any staff member may, at any time, for any reason, evaluate the Internet usage logs and e-mail files of any student or other staff member." Clearly, such a policy would make all users of the system feel uncomfortable.

The standards for school officials in conducting a search where there is a legitimate expectation of privacy were enunciated by the Supreme Court in the case of *New Jersey v. T.L.O, 469 U.S. 325* (1985). These standards are:

- Was the search "justified in its inception?" (*Id.* at *341*). A search is justified when there are "reasonable grounds for suspecting that the search would turn up evidence that the students has violated or is violating either the law or rules of the school" (*Id.* at *342*).
- Was the search "reasonably related in scope to the circumstances which justified the interference in the first place?" (*Id.* at *342*). A search is reasonable when "the measures adopted are reasonably related to the objectives of the search and not excessively intrusive in light of the age and sex of the student and the nature of the infraction" (*Id.* at *342*).

Most school districts have student search and seizure policies related to student lockers and desks that are in accord with the T.L.O. legal standards. The policies provide that a general inspection may occur on a regular basis, with advance notice to the students. Special inspections of individual lockers or desks may be conducted when there is reasonable suspicion to believe that illegal or dangerous items or items that are evidence of a violation of the law or school rules are contained in the locker or desk.

These same standards can be applied in the context of analysis of Internet usage records and e-mail files, as follows:

- Routine Supervision and Monitoring — Users should be provided with a notice that all use of the Internet will be supervised and monitored on a regular basis. Routine monitoring may be facilitated with the use of technical monitoring tools. Routine supervision may reveal instances of misuse that are in plain view.
- Individualized Searches — Special inspection of the online activities of an individual user should occur only when there are indicators that raise a reasonable suspicion that inappropriate activity has occurred or is occurring. The district should establish a process by which individualized searches of usage records are authorized. Most teachers and librarians are quite familiar with the types of "body language" exhibited by students that would give rise to a "reasonable suspicion" that misuse might be occurring. Such body language would justify an individualized analysis of the material present on the computer screen or listed in the history file.
- Instances Where There are No Expectations of Privacy — There also may be situations where there are no expectations of privacy. Use of a computer in the middle of the library or a computer lab

is a use where there should be no expectations of privacy because everything that the student is doing is in plain view of those passing by. Elementary student use of a classroom e-mail account is another situation where there are no expectations of privacy.

The Importance of Notice

The most important step a district must take is fully and completely informing all students and staff of what they can expect in terms of privacy. By providing notice of the degree to which use of the Internet is supervised and monitored, the district is allowing students to learn important aspects of the boundaries of personal privacy and how to govern personal behavior and communications based on the expectations established for a certain system and the level of privacy to be expected on that system. When students enter the workforce, they will most likely be using the Internet on a system where all employee communications and actions are monitored.

The following is recommended policy language that fits within the standards discussed previously.

> Users have a limited expectation of privacy in the contents of their personal files, communication files, and record of Web research activities on the district's Internet system. Routine supervision and monitoring, utilizing both technical monitoring systems and staff supervision, may lead to discovery that a user has violated district policy or the law. An individual search will be conducted if there is reasonable suspicion that a user has violated district policy or the law. Students' parents have the right to request to see the contents of their children's files and records. Staff is reminded that their communications are subject to Freedom of Information laws.

Sensitive or Controversial Information

An issue that is not fully resolved by the aforementioned discussion is addressing the interests of a student who seeks access to Web sites that present information that is sensitive or potentially controversial. For example, a student seeking information related to gender orientation in a highly conservative community may place himself or herself at risk by seeking access to such information on a monitored school system. This is the kind of situation for which there are no clear answers.

One approach, that is included in the author's book, *Computer Ethics, Etiquette, and Safety for the 21st Century Student*, is to warn students about the possible negative ramifications of seeking sensitive information on an Internet system that is closely monitored. Students who may face some risk if their search for sensitive information is discovered could be advised to seek such information on a system that is not so closely monitored, such as Internet access at the public library.

Another approach, that would be more complicated to accomplish, would be for a district to establish some form of "white list" of approved research sites that includes sites that address sensitive or controversial information presented in an appropriate manner for students and to guarantee that the district will not review any records of student access to these sites. This kind of an approach could be implemented in an environment where the district relies on a technical monitoring system that filters Internet traffic and reports on suspected misuse. Such a system would need to be configured not to report on any traffic related to approved sites.

Conclusion

Use of the Internet in school will clearly call upon school librarians to address situations that require a sophisticated analysis of ethics, as well as legal issues. Above all, school librarians should consider their responsibility to help prepare their students to make safe and responsible decisions when the use the Internet, regardless of where or how such access is obtained.

Works Cited

American Association of School Librarians. (1999). *Position statement on the confidentiality of library records*. Retrieved on March 6, 2003, from
<http://www.ala.org/aasl/positions/ps_libraryrecords.html>.

American Library Association, et al. v. United States, No. 01-1303 and 01-1332. In the United States District Court for the Eastern District of Pennsylvania. J.S. App. 1a-191a URL:
<http://www.paed.uscourts.gov/documents/opinions/02D0415P.HTM>

Board of Education, Island Trees Union Free School District No. 26 v Pico, 457 US 853, 1982.

Children's Internet Protection Act (CIPA) (42 U.S.C. 254).

Hester v. United States, 265 U.S. 57 (1924).

Katz v. United States, 389 U.S. 347 (1967).

National Research Council. (2002). *Youth, pornography, and the Internet* (Dick Thornburgh & Herbert S. Lin, eds.). Retrieved on March 4, 2003, from
<http://bob.nap.edu/html/youth_internet/>.

Rideout, V. et al. (2002). *See No Evil: How Internet Filters Affect the Search for Online Health Information Executive Summary*, Kaiser Family Foundation. Retrieved on March 6, 2003, from <http://www.kff.org/content/2002/3294/Internet_Filtering_exec_summ.pdf>.

U.S. Department of Education. (2002). *Internet Access in U.S. Public Schools Up for Seventh Straight Year, press release 9/24/2002*. Retrieved on March 4, 2003, from <http://www.ed.gov/PressReleases/09-2002/09242002b.html>.

United States v. Simons, 206 F.3d 392, 398 (4th Cir. 2000).

Discussion Questions

1. Considering the requirements of the Children's Internet Protection Act (CIPA), how can the librarian meet the ethical obligations of access?

2. The librarian deals with many sensitive and controversial issues in the course of the job. How can the Internet help or hinder meeting ethical obligations associated with sensitive information?

3. In what ways can educating students on safe and responsible Internet use enable the librarian to better meet the ethical obligations of the profession?

Chapter Ten

Ethics in Professional Relationships

By Frank Hoffman

The Nature and Purpose of Professional Ethics

As noted by Richard W. Severson in his book, *The Principles of Information Ethics*, the terms "morality" and "ethics" are used interchangeably by most individuals. He goes on to state that while this is considered acceptable, it can foster confusion regarding the purpose of ethics (Severson, 1997, 7). Whereas moral experiences tend to occur spontaneously (Severson employs the word "reflex" to describe them), ethics is more structured and deliberative in nature. The latter — a process of critically analyzing moral issues — is necessary for dealing with situations and issues that are new and/or complex to us (8).

From this perspective — that is, its use as a vehicle for applying measured thought processes to moral concerns — ethics is vital to professionals as a means of facilitating decision making in complicated situations. In pursuit of moral balance, the professional should cultivate the ability to debate and disagree within a public forum. The core value enabling us to cope — even flourish — in a world of differing ideas and ideals is civility. Civility requires that we be fair and charitable to those whose behavior and beliefs may be diametrically opposed to our own (Severson, 1997, 12).

Severson prescribes ethics — a working set of principles governing interpersonal communication and behavior — as a "booster shot" to:

- Help guide and educate our moral instincts;
- Steer us away from uncompromising positions; and
- Improve our moral vocabulary so that we might talk and listen better (Severson, 1997, 13).

Within a professional context, Severson recommends the following four-step method for using ethical principles as guidance in dealing with moral dilemmas arising in the workplace:

1. Get the facts straight.
2. Identify the moral dilemma (inspect the facts in light of your moral feelings).

3. Evaluate the moral dilemma using the principles of information ethics to decide which side has the most ethical support.
4. Test your solution: will it stand up to public scrutiny? (1997, 18).

The Library Professional Imperative

Although philosophers such as Aristotle, Spinoza, and Kant have written extensively on the role of ethics in everyday life, librarians — with the exception of terse discussions of etiquette and decorum — have been slow to adapt such principles to their own environment. Michael D. Bayles's three-point outline of ethical obligations represents a distillation of these philosophical theories within a professional context.

> First, come standards, which simply indicate that one should aspire to certain characteristics, e.g., knowledge, honesty, and competence. Standards are not prescriptive. Second are principles of responsibility. These obligations delimit, but still leave room for discretion, e.g., it is the responsibility of an information specialist to provide factually correct material, but the manner in which this is located and the sources used are discretionary. Finally, there are rules of duty. Here one is bound, perhaps even legally, to act in a specific way. For example, it is the duty of personnel to maintain the confidentiality of circulation records (1981, 22–23).

While primarily concerned with the professional-client paradigm, the Bayles model is applicable to the full range of relationships involving library professionals. In any of these situations, ethical problems arise when a combination of these obligations conflict with each other. More to the point, the problem is related to the absence of a clear-cut resolution to the conflict. Robert Hauptman argues, "no truly casuistic set of rules or regulations can provide for every contingency" (1998, 2). Consequently, morally responsible professional behavior — indeed, all human behavior — involves thoughtful deliberation of the available choices, complemented by the courage to take the responsibility for one's actions and decisions. Likewise, slavish adherence to the dictates of administrators, peers, professional organizations, and others possessing a vested interest in a given situation (e.g., parents of students, religiously-motivated activist groups) represents a compromise of an individual professional's moral imperatives.

Moral guidelines proscribing appropriate actions for library practitioners are needed due to the limited ability of governmental licensing agencies and professional associations to achieve compliance. Regarding the latter, Hauptman notes:

> It is certainly ironic that such a large, wealthy, and powerful organization as the ALA has absolutely no power over its members or over librarians generally. This is perhaps one of the greatest impediments to full professional status for librarians, at least in the eyes of laypersons. In librarianship, compliance with professional/ethical norms derives not from authority but rather from the individual's conscience—and since librarians are taught to demarcate professional activity from personal beliefs, ethical foundations are grounded in paradox. It is thus hardly surprising that, even today, ethical concerns are of no great import in schools of librarianship or in the workplace (1998, 7–8).

Likewise, peer pressure cannot be relied upon since consensus as to what constitutes ethical behavior will rarely be achieved. Consequently, only employers or legal authorities can compel compliance, and such controls generally apply to cases of clear-cut dishonesty or immorality (e.g., theft, vandalism, assault, sexual abuse).

With the exception of certain forms of special librarianship (e.g., information brokering, corporate information service), librarians — like teachers — profited for many years from a public trust halo effect derived from the nonprofit underpinnings of the service paradigm. However, while the ethical behavior of librarians may have been widely taken for granted, librarians — like professionals in other fields — are increasingly threatened by malpractice lawsuits. Accusations of malpractice have emanated from unethical activities in some cases; however, incompetence (particularly, inadequacies in reference service) appears more likely to be the precipitating factor behind future legal challenges centered on malpractice (Hauptman, 1998, 8).

Librarians are likely to mount a successful defense against many malpractice actions due to problems in discerning the fine line between irresponsible performance and the execution of professional duties — however poor — that still falls within the realm of legal acceptability. Nevertheless, the media coverage surrounding such suits will have other negative effects; most notably, an erosion of the public trust which has enabled librarians to set their own standards for professional behavior.

The Rise of Library Codes of Ethics

Codes of ethics represent a concerted effort on the part of a profession to address moral issues falling within its range of service imperative. Such documents relating to American librarianship, however, were slow to develop. According to Lindsey and Prentice, the issue "appears to have been irrelevant prior to 1900, and some would say that it has been of little relevance since" (1985, 19). Although Mary W. Plummer documented such concerns in 1903, the American Library Association remained silent until promulgating the 1939 Code of Ethics for Librarians. Due in part to its inherent weaknesses — excessive length, preoccupation with irrelevancies, failure to adequately address complex issues, and lack of enforceability — the document had little practical value to librarians (Hauptman, 1998, 5). ALA's "Statement on Professional Ethics" offered more precise language and a clear sense of the professional imperatives, but was also unenforceable and a poor anecdote to stressful situations (1975). The "Statement of Professional Ethics 1981" — consisting of a tersely-worded introduction which reiterated the profession's commitment to mutual cooperation, intellectual freedom, information access, and personal integrity and competence followed by the six-part Code of Ethics — updated the concerns governing decisions and actions within librarians' social and institutional environment.

ALA's 1995 Code of Ethics is presently the primary document stating the profession's "ethical responsibilities ... in this changing information environment." In addition to addressing quality service to clients, intellectual freedom, confidentiality, and copyright in the code proper, the last four statements comprising the code proper cover various aspects of professional relationships:

> V. We treat co-workers and other colleagues with respect, fairness and good faith, and advocate conditions of employment that safeguard the rights and welfare of all employees of our institutions.
>
> VI. We do not advance private interests at the expense of library users, colleagues, or out employing institutions.
>
> VII. We distinguish between out personal convictions and professional duties and do not allow our personal beliefs to interfere with fair representations of the aims of our institutions or the provision of access to their information resources.
>
> VIII. We strive for excellence in the profession by maintaining and enhancing our own knowledge and skills, by encouraging the professional development of coworkers, and by fostering the aspirations of potential members of the profession (ALA, 1995).

The School Library Perspective

School librarians differ from the profession at large in that they are also classified as educators. Therefore, accountability can be achieved through certification or licensing at the state level. Furthermore, many states have published codes of ethics to supplement professional standards (a sampling have been cited after the appended Works Cited). While the greater portion of these codes is devoted to the provision of fair and competent treatment of patrons (i.e., students), professional relationships are also covered in general terms. These relationships can be wide-ranging in nature, encompassing:

1. Site personnel
   a. Teaching professionals
   b. "Nonprofessional" staff, including clerks, maintenance workers, and so forth
   c. Administrators
2. District personnel
   a. Librarians at other sites
   b. Administrators, including line supervisors (superintendent, library/technology coordinators) and the School Board
3. Contacts at large
   a. Workshop speakers and other experts
   b. Visiting evaluators and observers
   c. Legal advisors
   d. Jobbers and service staff
   e. Mass media
   f. Student parents and community taxpayers

Beyond the cornerstone qualities of honesty and objectivity, regular, ongoing communication is essential to the development of ethical professional relationships with both organization personnel and outside contacts. In addition to traditional forms of communication, such as phones, memos, print newsletters, committee meetings, and the like, contemporary librarians have a wide array of new channels enabling them to interact with associates. These include e-mail, e-mail lists, Web sites, electronic bulletin boards, and more advanced forms of telecommunications, including interactive television, which is now widely employed in schools and universities. In short, school librarians must be *available* to others in order to function at maximum efficiency, whether it be assisting teachers in the development of lesson plans, delegating responsibilities to paraprofessional staff, briefing principals and other administrators on issues having long-term public relations implications (e.g., copyright, censorship), the planning of continuing education programs, sharing a human interest piece with local broadcast media, or briefing parents on the security measures and use etiquette relating to a newly implemented multimedia learning lab.

Professional school librarians generally fill a number of levels in the administrator-subordinate relationship. While answering to both site supervisors and district specialists (e.g., library/media and technology coordinators), they may possess line authority over other librarians, staff employees, and volunteers as well as functional responsibilities relating to additional school personnel. Amidst the profusion of media images depicting illegal and unethical professional conduct (Bogue, 1985, 138–140), Ronald Rebore argues "there is no issue more important in our contemporary times than *ethical behavior*" (Rebore, 2001, 356). This issue takes on considerable complexity in administrator-subordinate relationships that involve day-to-day decision making where the lines of appropriate behavior are somewhat blurred: the gray area. Human resources administrators are particularly vulnerable because their decisions affect people in that most important area of life: employment. Students are also affected because the quality of their education depends upon the quality of the people employed by a school district (333). Accordingly, Rebore has formulated three principles for the ethical management of school human resources.

First, the exercise of these responsibilities in making judgments for decisions, over time, will help an individual to determine the sort of person and human resources professional he or she wants to become. Any given decision usually does not determine an individual's central orientation as a person unless it is a decision of monumental significance such as deliberately committing a felony. Rather, someone is constantly in the state of becoming either a better person and professional or a person who gradually loses his or her integrity. Even inappropriate decisions about issues that might appear to be rather insignificant can chip away at the edges surrounding a person's central core of integrity.

Second, the decisions of school human resources administrators have a definite effect upon school districts as institutions.

The third principle is taken from the Declaration of Independence: "... all men are created equal, ... they are endowed by their creator with certain unalienable rights, that among these are life, liberty, and the pursuit of happiness." Any action by a school human resources administrator to show preferential treatment to certain people, groups, or companies is contrary to this principle. The human resources administrator has a duty to ensure that such rights are manifested not only in the daily actions of employees but also in the policy and procedural processes of the school district (Rebore, 2001, 333–334).

Charlotte Danielson has provided a rationale for programs supporting educators first entering the profession.

> ... in many settings, beginning teachers are presented with more challenging teaching assignments than their more experienced colleagues. They are frequently assigned the most preparations, the most challenging students, and no classroom of their own. Although these practices are unconscionable, they are widespread (in Villani, 2002, ix).

In her opinion, such policies contribute greatly to the high attrition rates among new teachers as well as issues of morale and professional competence. Susan Villani describes a wide range of mentoring models — including programs funded by school systems, peer assistance and review programs, state-funded programs, grant-funded projects, and alternatively funded programs — which illustrate the possibilities for assisting entry-level educators (Villani, 2002, 29–206).

Mentoring represents one of the more widely employed helping relationships within the school library. Whether constituting an internship or a device for incorporating new professionals, it can be a positive experience for both the mentor and novice staff member. On the one hand, the mentor provides invaluable advice and guidance regarding job responsibilities specific to the school district, such as the automated circulation system, book orders and new book processing, statistics for campus and district reports, coordinating book fairs, giving book talks, and programs promoting reading. The experienced librarian will typically derive benefits from mentoring activities as well. The mentor may find that daily contact with beginning librarians rekindles enthusiasm for the service imperatives of the profession through the introduction to new authors, innovative ideas associated with cutting-edge research, the latest state and national standards relating to school library programs, and the updated teaching methodologies and subject matter covered by the graduate library school curriculum (Camp & Graham, 2002).

Alfino and Pierce argue that the current climate of rapid technological and social change influence both the means by which we do our jobs and the definition and scope of our professions (1997, 5). They go on to posit, however, that these external sources of change are not the only forces behind the ethical dilemmas confronting librarians today.

Professions have their own dynamic for change. Professionals who gather at conferences year after year and develop new programs and initiatives for patron service and technical skill will inevitably uncover new challenges and questions. In the intellectual freedom movement of the early 1960s, librarians had to sort through the moral concerns of patrons who felt that children should not have unrestricted access to the "adult" collection. If librarians felt moral confusion, torn perhaps between values of open intellectual inquiry and paternalism, it was not a confusion caused so much by a new technology or changing social forces as by the very practices of librarianship (Alfino & Pierce, 1997, 6).

FamiliesConnect, the parent/extended family component of ALA's American Association of School Librarians' ICONnect technology initiative, has found a particularly creative approach to resolving the ethical complexities posed by present day Internet use in the schools. Its recently instituted online course, "Raising Good Citizens for a Virtual World: How Do We Help Our Children Be Safe and Ethical When Using the Internet?" attempts to constructively address community concerns within the context of the profession's traditional value system. Developed by Doug Johnson, Director of Media and Technology for the Mankato (Minnesota) Public Schools, the course (consisting of five lessons delivered to participants by e-mail) enables parents and other caregivers to more fully understand the appropriate behaviors in the face of threats and pitfalls, such as computer hacking, computer viruses, strangers possessed of dubious motives, readily accessible pornography, plagiarism, and personal privacy concerns (AASL, 2001).

Despite such promising initiatives and wealth of literature and research providing a library dimension for participatory management, employee orientation, and relationships with clients and allied professionals (e.g., educators, trustees, vendors), school librarians lag behind their colleagues employed by other types of libraries in many respects. Subject first and foremost to the political and professional climate created by education practitioners, they often find it difficult to garner support for the service imperatives developed within the library profession at large. Nevertheless, many school library programs exist as a testament to the fact that the application of sound ethical principles within a receptive environment can pay dividends for the community as a whole.

Works Cited

Alfino, M. and Pierce, L. (1997). *Information ethics for librarians.* Jefferson, NC: McFarland.

American Association of School Librarians. (2001). *New online course helps parents with ethical issues of Internet use.* Retrieved January 2001 from <http://www.ala.org/aasl/news/fcethicsfeb2001.html>.

American Library Association. (1995). *American Library Association code of ethics.* Retrieved December 2002, from <http://www.ala.org/alaorg/oif/ethics.htm>.

Bayles, M. D. (1981). *Professional ethics.* Belmont, CA: Wadsworth.

Bogue, E. G. (1985). *The enemies of leadership: lessons for leaders in education.* Bloomington, IN: Phi Delta Kappa Educational Foundation.

Camp, J., and Graham, M. (2002). [Notes on mentoring benefits compiled by two librarians employed within the Klein (TX) Independent School District]. Unpublished raw data.

Hauptman, R. (1998). *Ethical challenges in librarianship.* Phoenix: Oryx Press.

Lindsey, J. A., and Prentice, A. E. (1985). *Professional ethics and librarians.* Phoenix: Oryx Press.

Rebore, R. W. (2001). *Human resources administration in education: a management approach* (6th ed.). Boston: Allyn and Bacon.

Severson, R. W. (1997). *The principles of information ethics.* Armonk, New York: M.E. Sharpe.

Villani, S. (2002). *Mentoring programs for new teachers: models of induction and support.* Thousand Oaks, CA: Corwin.

School Codes of Ethics

California. "Rules of Conduct for Professional Educators, Title 5, Article 3." <http://www.vtusd.k12.ca.us/policy/id1010_m.htm>

Georgia. Professional Standards Committee. "Code of Ethics for Educators; Professional Practices — Rules." <http://www.gapsc.com/Professionalpractices/NEthics.asp>; <http://gapsc.com/Professionalpractices/Rules/505-6-.01.asp>

Iowa. Board of Educational Examiners. "Standards for Professional Practice and Competent Performance." <http://www.uni.edu/teached/students/ethics.html>

Kentucky. "Professional Code of Ethics for Kentucky School Certified Personnel." <http://dpi.state.nc.us/teacher_educatoin/conductcode.htm>

North Carolina. "Code of Professional Practice and Conduct for North Carolina Educators." <http://dpi.state.nc.us/teacher_education/conductcode.htm>

Discussion Questions

1. Many of the professionals who work in a school have independent codes of ethics. Most are obligated to multiple sets of ethical rules (e.g., teacher ethics and librarian ethics). At times, these ethical rules will conflict. What precedence should these rules take, and how does one resolve the areas of conflict?

2. Looking at the current Code of Ethics, what topics appear to be missing? What aspects need to be clarified or redefined?

3. Compare the ALA Code of Ethics with the teacher code of ethics for a teacher group of your choice. Do you see any conflicts in the ethical concepts? In the application of the ethical principles?

Appendix — Codes of Ethics

American Library Association

As members of the American Library Association, we recognize the importance of codifying and making known to the profession and to the general public the ethical principles that guide the work of librarians, other professionals providing information services, library trustees and library staffs.

Ethical dilemmas occur when values are in conflict. The American Library Association Code of Ethics states the values to which we are committed, and embodies the ethical responsibilities of the profession in this changing information environment.

We significantly influence or control the selection, organization, preservation, and dissemination of information. In a political system grounded in an informed citizenry, we are members of a profession explicitly committed to intellectual freedom and the freedom of access to information. We have a special obligation to ensure the free flow of information and ideas to present and future generations.

The principles of this Code are expressed in broad statements to guide ethical decision making. These statements provide a framework; they cannot and do not dictate conduct to cover particular situations.

I. **We provide the highest level of service to all library users through appropriate and usefully organized resources; equitable service policies; equitable access; and accurate, unbiased, and courteous responses to all requests.**

II. **We uphold the principles of intellectual freedom and resist all efforts to censor library resources.**

III. **We protect each library user's right to privacy and confidentiality with respect to information sought or received and resources consulted, borrowed, acquired or transmitted.**

IV. **We recognize and respect intellectual property rights.**

V. **We treat co-workers and other colleagues with respect, fairness and good faith, and advocate conditions of employment that safeguard the rights and welfare of all employees of our institutions.**

VI. **We do not advance private interests at the expense of library users, colleagues, or our employing institutions.**

VII. **We distinguish between our personal convictions and professional duties and do not allow our personal beliefs to interfere with fair representation of the aims of our institutions or the provision of access to their information resources.**

VIII. **We strive for excellence in the profession by maintaining and enhancing our own knowledge and skills, by encouraging the professional development of co-workers, and by fostering the aspirations of potential members of the profession.**

Adopted by the ALA Council, June 28, 1995. © Copyright 1997, 1998, 1999, 2000, 2001, 2002, American Library Association. The American Library Association is providing information and services on the World Wide Web in furtherance of its nonprofit and tax-exempt status. Permission to use, copy and distribute documents delivered from this World Wide Web server and related graphics is hereby granted for private, non-commercial and education purposes only, and not for resale, provided that the above copyright notice appears in all copies and that both that copyright notice and this permission notice appear. All other rights reserved. Reprinted with permission. <http://www.ala.org/Content/NavigationMenu/Our_Association/Offices/Intellectual_Freedom3/Statements_and_Policies/Code_of_Ethics/Code_of_Ethics.htm>

Association for Educational Communications and Technology Code of Ethics

Preamble

The Code of Ethics contained herein shall be considered to be principles of ethics. These principles are intended to aid members individually and collectively in maintaining a high level of professional conduct.

The Professional Ethics Committee will build documentation of opinion (interpretive briefs or ramifications of intent) relating to specific ethical statements enumerated herein.

Opinions may be generated in response to specific cases brought before the Professional Ethics Committee.

Amplification and/or clarification of the ethical principles may be generated by the Committee in response to a request submitted by a member.

Section 1—Commitment to the Individual

In fulfilling obligations to the individual, the members:

1. Shall encourage independent action in an individual's pursuit of learning and shall provide open access to knowledge regardless of delivery medium or varying points of view of the knowledge.
2. Shall protect the individual rights of access to materials of varying points of view.
3. Shall guarantee to each individual the opportunity to participate in any appropriate program.
4. Shall conduct professional business so as to protect the privacy and maintain the personal integrity of the individual.
5. Shall follow sound professional procedures for evaluation and selection of materials, equipment, and furniture/carts used to create educational work areas.
6. Shall make reasonable efforts to protect the individual from conditions harmful to health and safety, including harmful conditions caused by technology itself.
7. Shall promote current and sound professional practices in the appropriate use of technology in education.
8. Shall in the design and selection of any educational program or media seek to avoid content that reinforces or promotes gender, ethnic, racial, or religious stereotypes. Shall seek to encourage the development of programs and media that emphasize the diversity of our society as a multi-cultural community.

9. Shall refrain from any behavior that would be judged to be discriminatory, harassing, insensitive, or offensive and, thus, is in conflict with valuing and promoting each individual's integrity, rights, and opportunity within a diverse profession and society.

Section 2 — Commitment to Society

In fulfilling obligations to society, the member:

1. Shall honestly represent the institution or organization with which that person is affiliated, and shall take adequate precautions to distinguish between personal and institutional or organizational views.
2. Shall represent accurately and truthfully the facts concerning educational matters in direct and indirect public expressions.
3. Shall not use institutional or Associational privileges for private gain.
4. Shall accept no gratuities, gifts, or favors that might impair or appear to impair professional judgment, or offer any favor, service, or thing of value to obtain special advantage.
5. Shall engage in fair and equitable practices with those rendering service to the profession.
6. Shall promote positive and minimize negative environmental impacts of educational technologies.

Section 3 — Commitment to the Profession

In fulfilling obligations to the profession, the member:

1. Shall accord just and equitable treatment to all members of the profession in terms of professional rights and responsibilities, including being actively committed to providing opportunities for culturally and intellectually diverse points of view in publications and conferences.
2. Shall not use coercive means or promise special treatment in order to influence professional decisions or colleagues.
3. Shall avoid commercial exploitation of that person's membership in the Association.
4. Shall strive continually to improve professional knowledge and skill and to make available to patrons and colleagues the benefit of that person's professional attainments.
5. Shall present honestly personal professional qualifications and the professional qualifications and evaluations of colleagues, including giving accurate credit to those whose work and ideas are associated with publishing in any form.
6. Shall conduct professional business through proper channels.
7. Shall delegate assigned tasks to qualified personnel. Qualified personnel are those who have appropriate training or credentials and/or who can demonstrate competency in performing the task.
8. Shall inform users of the stipulations and interpretations of the copyright law and other laws affecting the profession and encourage compliance.
9. Shall observe all laws relating to or affecting the profession; shall report, without hesitation, illegal or unethical conduct of fellow members of the

profession to the AECT Professional Ethics Committee; shall participate in professional inquiry when requested by the Association.

10. Shall conduct research and practice using professionally accepted and institutional review board guidelines and procedures, especially as they apply to protecting human participants and other animals from harm. Humans and other animals shall not be used in any procedure that is physically invasive to them.

Reprinted with permission
<http://www.aect.org/About/Ethics.htm>

Useful Ethics Links

The American Bar Association has a listing of publications at
<http://www.abanet.org/abapubs/profresp.html>
California Rules of Conduct for Professional Educators:
<http://www.ventura.k12.ca.us/legalcounsel/id1010.htm>
Code of Ethics of the American Association of University Professors:
<http://www.aaup.org/statements/Redbook/Rbethics.htm>
Code of Ethics of the Canadian Library Association:
<http://www.cla.ca/about/ethics.htm>
Code of Ethics of the National Education Association:
<http://www.nea.org/code.html>
Code of Ethics of the National Association of Elementary School Principals:
<http://www.naesp.org/ethics.htm>
Code of Ethics of the American Association of School Administrators:
<http://www.aasa.org/about/ethics.htm>
Code of Ethics of the National Association of Secondary School Principals:
<http://www.principals.org/publicaffairs/stmnt_ethics.html>
Code of Professional Practice and Conduct for North Carolina Educators:
<http://www.ncpublicschools.org/teacher_education/conductcode.htm>
Georgia Code of Ethics for Educators; Professional Practices—Rules:
<http://www.gapsc.com/Professionalpractices/NEthics.asp>
How to write a code of ethics: <http://www.ethicsweb.ca/codes/>
Iowa Standards for Professional Practice and Competent Performance:
<http://www.uni.edu/teached/students/ethics.html>
Professional Code of Ethics for Kentucky School Certified Personnel:
<http://www.lrc.state.ky.us/kar/016/001/020.htm>
Professional Guidelines for the American Society for Information Science and Technology:
<http://www.asis.org/AboutASIS/professional-guidelines.html>
Writing a company's code of ethics: <http://www.iit.edu/departments/csep/perspective/persp_v19_fall99_5.html>

The Life We Lead

I've been reflecting on ethics lately.

I teach a course for school library media specialist students in which they're required to participate in an ethics simulation. The students read about several incidents involving illegal or unethical situations, ranging from out-and-out theft to subtle bribery to trendy influence peddling. Then they form groups and analyze these events from several viewpoints. It's always fun to watch students assess the hypothetical situations, because they all seem to think that they're more moral, more ethical than the typical person on the street, and that they certainly have higher principles than the average businessperson.

Yet, some of the same students who so loudly proclaimed their ethical superiority were found to have collaborated on class assignments even after explicit directions that they were to work independently. A couple of them even worked together on an exam, again, contrary to instructions. When confronted, these students first denied the accusation, then asserted that all they'd done was to share cataloging tool books and discuss cataloging theoretically, rather than answering individual test questions. Only when shown that their exams had identical, atypical errors did they even consider that what they'd done might have crossed the line into cheating. In the end, they never admitted that they'd done something wrong.

Another, more recent incident involved students who recycled papers from earlier courses, contrary to the student code of conduct, which states that a paper may not be "double-dipped," i.e., submitted in two different courses, without the express permission of the current professor. A quirk of fate allowed the discovery of the resubmission, but once the discovery had been made, the students were highly offended that their ethics were called into question. The professor explained that it wasn't fair that they should have to do only one-tenth the amount of work as their classmates did, yet get the same grade. In addition, the assignments from the earlier class and the current class were different, yet the students had made only minimal changes to their original work before resubmitting it for a fresh grade.

These incidents have prompted me to look with a new eye at our ethics of collaboration and partnership.

While these words appear noble and empowering, I'm finding that more and more librarians define "collaboration" as being a matter of simply appropriating certain material and combining it with other materials — to the end of not having to do much work themselves. This has become an intellectual property issue, an ethical issue, a moral issue. We would fail a student in a heartbeat if we had any inkling that the student had "borrowed" work from an older sibling or a neighbor who'd taken the class the year before. But we, ourselves, will assemble and even promote products in which we've invested very little time or effort. We tell students to "do your own work," but we model an ethic that's based on appropriation without acknowledgement. And we get angry when someone finds out. "Do as I say, not as I do" has become the mantra for teachers and media specialists. Is it a wonder, then, that when the tables are turned, and the teachers become the students, they experience a sudden sense of loss of control? All at once they must become independent creators, must demonstrate their personal expertise, must accept responsibility—and their behavior will be monitored and judged.

Ethics is a topic that extends far beyond revealing circulation records or resisting censorship. It's a matter of personal accountability, of thoughtful decision making, of resolute standards. Ethics is a matter of character, and if you don't have character by the time you get to graduate school, you aren't going to learn it there.

Reprinted from *Library Media Connection*, March 2003. Vol 21, No. 6, p.8.

A Hat Trick

DATE

Ethics. A word of great mystery. Lately it seems that it is a term whose definition is in flux. Sometimes the definition is determined by the person who doesn't want to be cornered into doing something he doesn't want to do. At other times, it is defined by someone who doesn't want to be caught doing something he shouldn't. Seldom are ethics discussed prior to a "situation."

The trouble with ethics in librarianship is that school librarians, in particular, wear so many different hats. Each hat has its own ethical framework, and the frames don't always fit together well. Most school librarians were teachers at one time, and they absorbed the ethic of teaching. Many teaching practices are designed to facilitate the bureaucracy of the school more than create an individually customized learning environment. Peer grading, posting student work, rewarding student work with recreational videos, etc. all fit with the teaching-as-assembly-line ethic. Enter the librarian hat. The librarian is anxious to provide just the right learning resource at just the right learning moment. The librarian protects the patron, even one underage, from idle curiosity about reading habits. The librarian personally follows, and creates an environment in which others may comply with, copyright law. Can one hat fit with the other? Which is the most important hat to wear?

In a student's K–12 career, he or she will have many teachers—maybe three dozen. Many people will tease, instruct, cajole, threaten, encourage, and evaluate his or her progress. In the same academic career, the student will have perhaps four librarians. While the librarian is there to support the student's academic career, he or she is also there to give look after recreational and personal needs. He or she protects the student's curiosity while feeding it. He or she defends the student's right to read, to view, to listen, to speak in ways that the classroom teacher never can. There are many classroom teachers in a building. There is usually one librarian.

When it comes time to speak for the student, there are many classroom teachers to take the teacher's viewpoint. There is one librarian. Sometimes the librarian's voice is timid, but it must be heard. The classroom teacher, the counselor, the principal, or even the child's parents will not voice the ethical viewpoint of the library media specialist. The spirit of intellectual freedom and inquiry lives in the ethical foundations of librarianship. It is one voiced by the founding fathers in the first amendment to the U.S. Constitution. If you haven't taken a look at the Code of Ethics for librarianship lately, maybe it is time for a refresher. This is the beginning of a new school year. It can be a new era in your professional development. Look at the hat rack in the corner. Which is yours?